SELF-CARE IN SOCIAL WORK

A Guide for Practitioners, Supervisors, and Administrators

Kathleen Cox and Sue Steiner

Jeane W. Anastas, PhD, LMSW
President

Elizabeth J. Clark, PhD, ACSW, MPH
Executive Director

NASW PRESS

National Association of Social Workers
Washington, DC 20002-4241

Cheryl Y. Bradley, *Publisher*
John Cassels, *Project Manager and Staff Editor*
Lisa M. O'Hearn, *Copyeditor*
Lori J. Holtzinger, *Indexer*

Cover by Eye to Eye Design Studio
Interior design and composition by Electronic Quill Publishing Services
Printed and bound by Sheridan Books, Inc.

© 2013 by the NASW Press

First impression: March 2013

Library of Congress Cataloging-in-Publication Data

Cox, Kathleen (Kathy)
   Self-care in social work: a guide for practitioners, supervisors, and administrators / Kathleen Cox and Sue Steiner.
        p. cm.
   Includes bibliographical references and index.
   ISBN 978-0-87101-444-3
   1. Social workers. 2. Social service. I. Steiner, Sue. II. Title.
   HV40.35.C683 2012
   361.3—dc23

                                                                    2012013558

Printed in the United States of America

Table of Contents

About the Authors

Kathleen (Kathy) Cox, PhD, LCSW, is an associate professor at the School of Social Work at California State University, Chico. She earned her MSW from San Diego State University and her doctorate from the University of Southern California. She previously worked as a licensed practitioner, clinical supervisor, and administrator in the field of children's mental health. Kathy currently teaches a variety of courses in social work practice, practicum, and research. The focus of her scholarship is strength-based assessment and intervention with high-risk families, traumatic stress, and self-care for helping professionals.

Sue Steiner, PhD, MSW, is a professor at the school of Social Work at California State University, Chico. Over the years, she has taught community practice, program development, grant-writing, research, social welfare policy, and field practicum courses. Sue has worked in community organization, social welfare policy, and organizational development. She is the coauthor of *An Introduction to the Profession of Social Work* (3rd ed.) (Brooks Cole, 2009), and her current scholarship focuses on effective teaching methods.

Acknowledgments

We express our gratitude to the human service workers, supervisors, and administrators who made this book possible. We thank all of the agencies that invited us to conduct workshops and focus groups on the topic of stress and self-care. They took a risk by approving a forum through which employees could share the hardships they endure in the workplace. We also thank all the participants in our groups for their honesty in revealing the realities of their day-to-day experience on the job. We are especially grateful to the individuals who provided us with their written stories as they relate to stressful encounters and successes that they have experienced in the field. The students who have participated in our courses over the years have also provided us with tremendous insight into the challenges related to the work we do. We appreciate their willingness to share their experiences and help us continue to learn.

We thank the Office of Research and Sponsored Programs at California State University, Chico for providing us with a grant that supported our project. We very much appreciate the NASW Press and John Cassels for supporting and enhancing our work. We also value the support and wisdom shared by colleagues in our School of Social Work as it relates to stress and self-care. Finally, we thank our family and friends who supported us by listening to ideas and sharing suggestions.

Sue would like to offer special thanks to Dilia Loe, who generously offered insights from her years of experience in guiding organizations and continues to bring deep wisdom, humor, and compassion into her life. Kathy would like to thank her children—Aaron, Jack, and Kayla—for inspiring her, keeping her grounded, and helping her see the humor in most of what life brings.

Editorial Note

This book contains information and true accounts that may stir strong emotions in the reader. Stories shared and illustrations provided are sometimes graphic and disturbing. Our intent is to provide an honest portrayal of the traumatizing and stressful circumstances that professional helpers frequently face. It may be important for readers to pace themselves as they absorb this material. Our overall aim, however, is to reveal the coping ability of social workers and strategies for self-care that have proven to be effective. We include many examples of the ways in which practitioners, supervisors, and agencies manage the stress involved with a highly challenging yet rewarding occupation.

Preface

Our study of self-care in the helping professions has just begun. It started with a desire to support our undergraduate and graduate students in social work who lamented the lack of time for self-care and a limited understanding of what is really meant by the term. We had heard comments such as, "You guys are always telling us that self-care is important but you load us up with so much work that we have no time for it! What is self-care anyway?" Such questions and concerns sparked our interest in developing a thorough understanding of self-care and the ways in which it can be embedded in all that we do as social workers. We were of the opinion that it should not be an afterthought or an add-on to other more important responsibilities. To learn more, we went to the experts: workers in the human services field who have insight into not only the stress of social work, but also what constitutes effective workplace coping. We recruited over sixty of them to participate in workshops and focus groups to explore this issue in depth. In addition, we asked colleagues and students to send us stories that reflect their experiences with various workplace challenges and reviewed the literature across disciplines that address biological, psychological, social, cultural, spiritual, and organizational aspects of stress and coping.

Our work in this area continues. To further understanding of self-care, we invite reader participation. We ask that you reflect on the material presented here and share your reactions with us. We would appreciate hearing about your first-hand experiences with the various forms of trauma, distress, and difficulty discussed in the chapters to follow, as well as your approaches to self-care. We have constructed a Web site that offers a mechanism for sharing your story, anonymously if you prefer. Our hope is that the Web site will facilitate information sharing, support, and communication within the social work community as it concerns this important topic. Please visit http://www.selfcareinsocialwork.com.

Introduction

Many social workers enter the profession because they have a desire to help others in need and contribute to the betterment of society. They are drawn to a line of work wherein they can assist individuals, groups, families, and communities to surmount the hardships and challenges that life brings. New to their craft, these budding professionals are fully prepared to use their hard-earned knowledge and to hone their skills to attain the rewards that are promised by a people-oriented practice. What comes as a surprise to some, however, is the huge toll that the work takes on social workers' emotional well-being, physical health, and interpersonal functioning over the course of their, sometimes short, careers.

Leaders in the field of social work are now calling attention to the sometimes serious consequences of work-related stress on individuals and the systems in which they are employed. Figley (1995) coined the term *compassion fatigue*, in referring to a set of physical and psychological symptoms appearing in social workers who are exposed to client suffering that occurs as a result of traumatizing events such as physical or sexual abuse, combat, domestic violence, or the suicide or unexpected death of a loved one. Psychological symptoms of this type of secondary traumatic stress include depression, anxiety, fear, rage, shame, emotional numbing, cynicism, suspiciousness, poor self-esteem, and intrusive thoughts or avoidance of reminders about client trauma. Physiological symptoms, including hypertension, sleep disruption, and immune system malfunctions, have been found to result in serious illness and a relatively high mortality rate in helping professionals (Beaton & Murphy, 1995). Similarly, *burnout* has been defined as a process involving gradually increasing emotional exhaustion in workers, along with a negative attitude toward clients and reduced commitment to the profession (Maslach, 1993). It is thought to be associated with a work environment that makes

1

high demands on employees but offers limited supports and rewards. Both worker burnout and secondary traumatic stress have been implicated in high rates of turnover in social work organizations (Pryce, Shakelford, & Pryce, 2007). Another occupational hazard in the field of social work is referred to as *vicarious trauma*—a transformation of the professional helper's worldview as a result of "empathic engagement with survivor clients and their trauma material" (Sakvitne & Pearlman, 1996, p. 17). Because social workers are routinely exposed to client suffering and trauma, they may be vulnerable to shifts in their fundamental assumptions concerning safety, trust, control and benevolence in the world.

In response to these threats to the stability of social workers and the human service agencies in which they are employed, administrators may offer training seminars that provide education on the signs and symptoms of secondary traumatic stress. Coursework on this topic is also increasingly common in university curricula at both the undergraduate and graduate levels. These advances have built awareness of psychological risks within the profession, but they have offered limited assistance to social work interns and practitioners who are striving to resolve work-related distress and trauma. Training participants are often encouraged to practice "self-care," yet they are provided minimal guidance in conceptualizing this crucial process that promises both self-preservation and professional goal attainment. Moreover, suggestions offered for promoting personal care are often found to be of limited use or effectiveness. For instance, workers under mounting stress might be advised to "take breaks" from case-related or administrative tasks during their assigned shifts. After doing so, they might find that they are farther behind and feeling buried under unfulfilled duties and unmet expectations. Or distressed workers attempting to follow the recommendation to relax at home might find that instead of "leaving work behind" they are ruminating about mistakes made on the job and unaddressed client needs. They may also be checking e-mail from home, noting what is not getting done, and thus increasing their stress. Even more discouraging, the employee who accesses a therapist from his or her agency's employee assistance program may discover that the clinician has no understanding of these particular work-related issues.

This book offers an alternative to social work practitioners and interns seeking to understand the essential elements of self-care. It suggests a new way of thinking about how they can help themselves to function optimally on the job. In conceptualizing the process of self-care, we emphasize the importance of three "S"s: self-awareness, self-regulation, and self-efficacy. In addition to this microsystem focus on personal strategies for self-care, we incorporate a macrosystem perspective that recognizes organizational sources of stress and constructive coping. Because of this wide frame of reference, the intended audience of this book is quite broad and includes social work students, practitioners, supervisors, and administrators. In addition to serving as a guide for practicing social workers, this book is structured so that it may be used as a text for undergraduate and graduate social work practice and practicum courses and courses dedicated to understanding and reducing stress and improving self-care.

In presenting our views of self-care, we draw from the literature, statements made by participants in workshops and focus groups, and stories submitted by students and social workers about their experiences with work-related stress and strategies for coping. To facilitate the integration of material presented, we provide activities and examples, discussion questions, and chapter exercises. We encourage readers to take the time to read the *From the Field* stories and to carefully consider the questions posed in the sections titled "Reader Reflections." Discussion questions and exercises at the end of each chapter can be used in classes or workshop training sessions to help students and workers delve more deeply into the concepts discussed. We also invite readers to visit our Web site at www.selfcareinsocialwork.com, download worksheets and other activities and tools, and share their own experiences as they relate to the stress and coping in social work.

Part I of this book is aimed at conceptualizing the stress and coping process. Chapter 1 examines the effects of stress on our physiological, emotional, and behavioral functioning. It also highlights the importance of recognizing both personal and organizational sources of stress. Consistent with this dual focus, we assert that responsibility for the management of workplace stress lies both with the individual employee and the agency's management team or administration. Chapter 2 focuses on the ways in which the concept of self-care has evolved in recent years. We describe various commonly proposed strategies for self-care strategies, including those falling into the general categories of lifestyle or workplace adjustments.

Part II of the book delves into the three "S"s: self-awareness, self-regulation, and self-efficacy. Chapter 3 seeks to help readers become more aware of signs of stress, emotional reactions, and thinking patterns as they relate to social work. Particular emphasis is placed on situational meaning that may be derived from work-related experiences, including thoughts concerning client, self-, and system limitations. Chapter 4 is devoted to assisting social workers striving to regulate their emotions in response to clients who are needy, demanding, hostile, or distraught. The cognitive reframe is introduced as a valuable tool that reorients our perceptions of problematic events so that they are seen in a more positive light. In addition, the practice of mindfulness is discussed as a method of self-soothing for workers who are fatigued or "soul sick" as a result of empathic engagement with clients. This chapter also stresses the value of balance in the helping professions. It references an ancient Hindu myth ("Shiva's Circle") to illustrate the importance of balance between empathy toward others and a need to stand apart from their pain. Chapter 5 highlights threats to self-efficacy that are common in social work when client progress is painfully slow or nonexistent. It offers strategies for maintaining self-confidence and a sense of competence amid client resistance to change and slow systems change. For instance, we encourage workers to notice and celebrate small steps toward client success and system transformation. We also emphasize the importance of adapting case-based and professional goals so that they are realistic and achievable.

Part III of the book focuses on organizational issues as they relate to self-care. Chapter 6 aids readers in assessing their level of fit with their organization's culture as it concerns hierarchy, individualism, importance of relationships, directness of communication, time perspective, and information processing. It also suggests practical steps that can be taken to improve congruence between the individual's approach to managing work-related responsibilities and those favored by his or her organization. Chapter 7 stresses the importance of high-quality supervision in supporting the self-care of workers and in counteracting contagion, or the spread of traumatic stress within the agency. It also addresses stressors commonly experienced by supervisors. Finally, chapter 8 identifies structural steps that social work agencies can take to reduce employee stress and promote workplace wellness. In that chapter, we make a case for the devotion of organizational resources to the self-care of human service workers. We show how this results in benefits for both individual employees and the organization as a whole. Furthermore, we maintain that the future of the social work profession depends on the maintenance of a vibrant, healthy, and well-functioning workforce.

PART I
Understanding Stress and Self-Care

Chapter 1
Making Sense of Stress

Imagine yourself belonging to a band of hunter–gatherers who lived thousands of years ago. You are searching for nuts and fruits in an open field when a wild cat appears and fixes its gaze upon you. Your body immediately goes into overdrive. Your heart rate increases, your blood pressure rises, and your muscles contract. You race away from the predator at lightning speed. Now fast forward to the present day. Consider occasions in your life in which your body has produced a similar stress response. Were you in acute danger? Was the possibility of death imminent? Chances are that many of the events that have prompted this type of stress reaction did not involve a serious threat to your physical survival. Perhaps, instead, these events threatened your social and emotional well-being. According to Sapolsky (1998), this awareness is key to understanding stress and stress-related disease. He contended that when faced with a psychological stressor, our bodies mobilize a stress response that is almost identical to that of a jungle animal or early Homo sapiens who has encountered a life-threatening physical crisis. Over time, such psychologically induced yet biologically based stress reactions can make us ill. However, we can learn how to manage these responses and buffer ourselves from various forms of psychological stress. Thus, we can free ourselves from chronic suffering and pain, while increasing the likelihood of success in our personal and professional roles. To provide a foundation for this focus, we turn to the knowledge base concerning stress and coping that has evolved substantially over recent decades.

What Is Stress?

The term *stress* has been used for centuries to refer to hardship and adversity (Rutter, 1983). However, it was not until the 19th century that it was seen as the basis of ill health (Hinkle, 1977). Cannon (1932) has been credited for laying the groundwork for the systematic study of the effects of stress on the body. As early as 1932, he used the term to refer to a disturbance of homeostasis in the organism that is produced by conditions of pain, hunger, cold, and so on. Selye broadened this definition in the mid-1930s when he described stress as a "set of bodily defenses against any form of noxious stimulus" (Lazarus & Folkman, 1984, p.2). Selye believed that psychological as well as biological threats could serve as harmful agents that trigger a physiological set of reactions and processes. This new perspective helped to spread interest in the concept of stress from the field of physiology to the behavioral and social sciences.

Sociologists have focused on both the societal causes and consequences of stress. Durkheim (1893) addressed a primary cause of stress when he wrote about the alienation that arises when people experience a lack of norms to guide their efforts to achieve socially valued goals. In the 1950s, Seeman (1959) specified five causes of alienation, including powerlessness, meaninglessness, normlessness, isolation, and self-estrangement. More recently, Lazarus and Cohen (1977) identified three types of social or environmental events that trigger stress: major changes affecting many people (natural disasters, war, large scale relocation), major changes affecting few people (death of a loved one, loss of employment, divorce), and daily hassles (small things that irritate people). Other contemporary sociologists identified forms of social disruption that are thought to be the result of stress or strain, such as riots, panics, hate crimes, and other types of hostile outbursts (Smelser, 1963).

Psychologists have discovered that there are individual differences in the way that people respond to stressful circumstances. For instance, under the same mounting pressures, one person might respond with guilt or anxiety, whereas another might react with anger, and yet another might view the situation as an opportunity versus a threat. Lazarus and Folkman (1984) argued that it is important to understand the *cognitive,* or thinking processes, that mediate between a stressor and the individual's response. In fact, they proposed a model for conceptualizing the stress and coping process that highlights the role of the *cognitive appraisal.* This appraisal involves categorizing an event with regard to its significance to safety, security, and well-being. Stress appraisals are said to focus on *harm* (damage that has already been sustained), *threat* (harm that has not yet occurred but is expected), or *challenge* (potential for gain or growth as a result of the experience). Of these, only challenge appraisals dispose us to *eustress,* or the positive affect and excitement that we feel when we are confronted with a demanding situation that we believe we can handle (McGowan, Gardner, & Fletcher, 2006).

The definition of stress used in this book emphasizes the relationship between the individual and his or her social environment. Consistent with the Lazarus and Folkman (1984) model, psychological stress is viewed as a process that occurs when an environmental event is appraised by the person "as taxing or exceeding his or her resources and endangering his or her well-being" (p. 21). In the pages to follow, we examine personal factors that influence social workers' responses to workplace stressors. We also identify organizational factors that contribute to high levels of occupational stress.

How Stress Affects Us

When a frightening stimulus presents itself, a 90-second window opens. During this brief period of time, the brain releases chemicals that surge through the body, producing an automatic physiological experience. This fight or flight response results in elevations in heart rate, blood pressure, and blood sugar, with increased blood flow from essential organs to the muscles. Within 90 seconds from the original trigger, the chemical basis of the fear dissipates. At this point, one can make a choice to manage the emotions or let the neurological circuit continue to run (Bolte Taylor, 2006). When this stress response is prolonged or activated repeatedly by psychological stressors, a persistent and harmful effect is exerted on your body. Overtime, such chronic distress can result in immune suppression, muscle atrophy, and, ultimately, "diseases of civilization," including diabetes, obesity, hypertension, heart attacks, and skin-related afflictions, such as psoriasis (Pandy, Campbell Quick, Rossi, Nelson, & Martin, 2010, p. 141).

In addition to these physiological effects, behavioral outcomes of chronic stress are recognized by researchers. High-level workplace stress is linked to impulsivity, lowered tolerance toward others, and aggression—both verbal and physical (Vigoda, 2002). Workplace stress also results in what has been termed *counterproductive work behavior,* such as lack of cooperation, withholding of effort, lying, theft, or sabotage (Penny & Spector, 2005, p. 777). Escalating job stress may also manifest in restlessness and agitation, overreaction to minor events, social withdrawal, and increased use of alcohol and drugs (Anschuetz, 1999).

Burnout is a relatively frequent outcome of chronic stress that has received considerable attention. The concept of burnout draws on a vivid

How Long Do You Hang on to Stress?

Imagine yourself in the situations described below. Would you be inclined to hang onto your stress for several hours or more, or would you let it go more quickly?

- You were stuck in an unavoidable traffic jam and therefore late for an important meeting at work. As you enter the meeting room everyone there, including your boss, turns and notices your late arrival. The facilitator of the meeting appears visibly annoyed. Would you explain the reason for your tardiness and then let it go, focusing your attention on the tasks at hand? Would you simmer through the meeting, wondering what consequences you will pay for being late? Would you let this event ruin your day and perhaps your evening?
- You had taken the time early this morning to make your lunch—a carefully prepared sandwich, a piece of your favorite fruit, and two small cookies. When you got to work you had placed your bagged lunch in the refrigerator in the break room. Now it is noon and you are hungry. You open the refrigerator only to find that your bag is open and the sandwich and cookies are gone! You ask around, but no one admits to having taken it or seeing anyone else who did. Would you laugh it off and get lunch elsewhere? Would you likely be angry and upset about this all day? Would you make it your goal to determine who had taken your lunch over the weeks to come? What would it take for you to overcome your stress about this situation?
- Your 8-year-old daughter's teacher calls you at work. She explains that your child was "accidentally" elbowed by another child on the playground. She goes on to report that the injury doesn't appear to be serious, although your daughter is upset about the fact that she has a black eye and needs to be picked up from school. You cancel your afternoon appointments and tell your boss that you need to leave work to take care of a "personal matter." Would you race to the school anxiously and then calm down once you saw that your daughter was OK? Would you hang on to your stress for the remainder of the day and ruminate about whether the event was really an accident? Would you worry for days to come that your daughter might be injured again? At what point could you put this incident behind you?

metaphor—one that depicts the "smoldering of a fire or the extinguishing of a candle" (Schaufeli, Leiter, & Maslach, 2009, p. 205). It refers to the gradual draining of energy that has occurred for the social worker who was once "on fire," but who is now emotionally and physically exhausted. Burnout is rooted in an organizational environment that is characterized by high work demands, low personal rewards, and minimum support (Freudenberger,

1974). According to Maslach and Leiter (2005a), it results from a lack of fit between a person and his or her job across six main areas. These include the following:

- workload (excessive work with inadequate resources),
- control (little influence, high levels of accountability with limited power),
- reward (low pay, recognition, or satisfaction),
- community (social isolation, interpersonal conflict),
- fairness (inequity, preferential treatment), and
- values (little sense of purpose or meaning, ethical conflicts).

As burnout progresses, it can produce callous attitudes, cynicism, and a negative evaluation of one's own personal effectiveness on the job. Ample research has linked burnout in social workers to turnover and intention to leave the job (Mor Barak, Nissly, & Levin, 2001).

Reader Reflections

1) Do you see signs of burnout in workers at your agency?
2) What organizational conditions may contribute to burnout in your workplace?
3) What aspects of the agency environment serve to protect workers from burnout?

Another cost of caring for the helping professional is referred to as *compassion fatigue* or *secondary traumatic stress* (STS). Both terms have been used to describe a set of behaviors and emotions that can naturally occur when the social worker seeks to help a traumatized or suffering person (Figley, 1995). This syndrome manifests in a variety of symptoms that cluster in three core areas: intrusion, avoidance, and arousal. Symptoms of intrusion include unexpected thoughts about one's clients, disturbing dreams about them, and a sense of reliving their traumatic experiences. Avoidance involves efforts to keep clear of clients or client reminders. It may also result in an inability to recall client information, diminished activity level, detachment from others, and emotional numbing. Symptoms of arousal include sleep disturbance, irritability, difficulty concentrating, hypervigilance, and an exaggerated startle response. In a recent study of the prevalence of STS in social workers, Bride (2007) found that 70% of those surveyed had at least one of these symptoms, at least occasionally, in the week prior to the survey. In addition, 55% of respondents met the criteria for at least one of three core symptom

From the Field: Bumping Into Burnout

During my first week on the job at a public agency, the training coordinator met with me. I was expecting her to orient me to my new position and give me information about my new organization. Instead, she spent most of our time together explaining how many people leave agency and how short their careers are. She went on to let me know that a majority of my colleagues were dealing with chronic fatigue and exhaustion. Many were on psychotropic medications for anxiety, depression, and trouble sleeping because of the demands of the job and conflicts with their coworkers. I wondered if these were known facts and also what the agency was doing to help address this. It did not take me long to realize that the existence of burnout was real and that the agency did little to address the problem. I personally observed several workers crying in the office or having emotional flare-ups. I came to know others who were ambivalent, caught between wanting to escape from the situation and an obsession to move forward with their case-carrying responsibilities. It is sad to say, but rather than look at the larger problem or come together, many workers were turning on one another and getting caught up in petty issues that only made the work environment more unpleasant. I also discovered that it was almost an unspoken rite of passage when a new social worker made it past the two-year marker in the agency! It was also clear that the seasoned social workers were tired of spending time and talent training new workers who ended up leaving so soon. This was a rude awakening to the realities of a field that I worked so hard to enter. I wasn't prepared to see this side of social work.

—*LeAnna*

clusters. The most commonly reported individual symptoms were intrusive thoughts, avoidance of client reminders, and numbing responses.

Finally, *vicarious traumatization* (VT) is conceptualized as an altered worldview that may occur for social workers who empathically engage with the trauma of their clients. As proposed by Pearlman and Saakvitne (1995), VT is seen as a cumulative transformation that occurs across time and helping relationships. It is said to result in disrupted beliefs and assumptions about self and others as they relate to trust, safety, control, esteem, and intimacy. The concept of vicarious trauma has a strong theoretical foundation in constructivist self-development theory—a conceptual framework focused on the ways in which individuals make meaning of their experiences. Although there is limited research regarding the prevalence of VT, anecdotal reports of this condition are relatively common. For instance, during workshops conducted

From the Field: Burdened with Burnout

I had worked for many years in the medical social work field and decided that I needed a change. So I took a job doing assessments and group work at a private psychiatric partial-hospitalization program. This program was owned and operated by a psychiatrist who was well-known in the community as a competent physician. However, as I came to understand in the years to follow, he had little or no leadership skill or management ability. He had very high expectations of his employees, but he offered little in the way of recognition for a job well done. None of the therapists ever received performance reviews or salary increases. To make matters worse, he and his assistant director piled on the work. The caseloads were completely unmanageable and documentation requirements were excessive. I found myself working after hours just to keep up. Eventually, I noticed that I was absolutely drained. I dreaded getting up in the morning and going to work. When I was at home, I was thinking about how much I hated my job. I was also cranky and irritable with my wife. She wanted to spend time with me but I had little energy to invest in the relationship. One day, I even lost my cool with the assistant director when he started in with his nit-picking and micromanagement. That's when I knew something had to give. I finally left this job and went back to a social work position in a medical hospital. It became clear to me that the novelty of working in a new area of social work was not worth the price I had been paying.

—Joe

with child welfare workers across five states, Pryce, Shakelford, and Pryce (2007) found that many described a shift in worldview that resulted from knowing about the terrible things that abused and neglected children experience. Some acknowledged their own loss of innocence, trust, companionship, and intimacy because of their daily encounters on the job. Similarly, Gold (1998) conducted focus groups with 40 child welfare workers to explore the effect of this work on their physical and emotional functioning. Some participants reported that their lives had been invaded by pessimism, jaded attitudes, and mistrust of people. One worker is quoted as stating, "I don't see the world with any normalcy any more. I only see it through the eyes of child abuse" (Gold, 1998, p. 712).

These accounts of chronic stress are quite alarming, perhaps even distressing in and of themselves. However, despite these potential pitfalls, many human service workers do not fall prey to serious work-related stress disorders. In fact, some fare quite well and manage to survive and even thrive in a very demanding and challenging occupation. These high-functioning professionals appear to know the art of self-care, in one or more of its variations, which is discussed in chapters to follow. It is also likely that they have received support in understanding and surmounting both personal and organizational sources of stress in social work.

Personal Sources of Stress

Consider two social workers who have encountered the same workplace stressor. Each has been made aware of a series of negative outcomes with the clients they have served over the last year—high service drop-out rates, limited goal attainment, and low client satisfaction with services. Worker 1 views this feedback as an indication that he or she is incompetent and should change occupations. Worker 2 perceives the poor outcomes as fixable and focuses on ways to turn things around. The latter employee considers a variety of external factors that could account for these outcomes, including inadequate screening of referrals, poor coordination among services providers, and increased caseloads. Now imagine that these same individuals have instead experienced a positive event: Each has been nominated as social worker of the month within their organizations. Worker 1 attributes this honor to the chance occurrence that he or she has pleased the supervisor in recent weeks, who is now merely trying to motivate him or her to work harder. Conversely, Worker 2 assumes that the nomination is a well-deserved recognition of his or her on-going hard work and capability. It can be said that these workers have different *attributional styles,* resulting in markedly dissimilar responses to both positive and negative situations. According to Peterson and Seligman (1984), attributional styles are reflected in the ways that circumstances and events are interpreted and explained. A person who adopts a negative attributional style tends to assume that the causes of problematic events are stable, internal, and universal, and that the causes of positive events are unstable, external, and situation-specific. The reverse is true of the person who embraces a positive attributional style. This individual tends to believe that negative events can be explained by factors that are temporary, external, and situation-specific, whereas positive events are caused by factors that are lasting, internal, and global. In a recent study with 190 nurses in a medical facility for veterans, Welbourne, Eggerth, Hartley, Andrew, and Sanchez (2007) linked a negative attributional style to the use of avoidant versus problem-solving approaches to dealing with workplace stress and to lower levels of job satisfaction. It has also been associated with depression (Seligman & Nolen-Hoeksema, 1987), health-related problems, and mortality (Peterson, Seligman, & Valliant, 1988).

Reader Reflections

1) Do you tend toward a positive or negative attributional style?
2) What life experiences have you had that may have shaped your style for interpreting and explaining both positive and problematic events?

Social work employees are also more vulnerable to stress on the job when they possess lower levels of *psychological hardiness*. Kobasa (1979) theorized that individuals with a hardy personality have a strong sense of commitment (purpose and meaning), control (belief that they can influence events), and challenge (orientation toward change as an opportunity for growth). In contrast, people with low levels of hardiness tend to feel uninvolved, powerless, and threatened as a result of their work-related experiences. As a result, they are likely to become uncooperative, inefficient, unmotivated, and might even succumb to stress-related illness (Lambert, Lambert, & Yamase, 2003). Understanding the components of psychological hardiness may be useful in the proactive management of workplace stress.

Another personal factor that appears to be related to occupational stress is *social identity*. The theory of social identity suggests that a person's sense of self is influenced by the knowledge that he or she belongs to a certain group (for example, social workers, case managers, clinicians) and not to others (for example, physicians, psychologists, administrators). This in-group–out-group identification is said to play a major role in determining whether a given stressor is seen as threatening (Haslam & van Dick, 2011). For example, an agency's adoption of a new evidence-based model of social work practice may be seen as a welcome change to administrators who are striving to improve agency outcomes and obtain a competitive edge with funders. Conversely, this step may be viewed as much more threatening to social work clinicians who have established their professional identity on the basis of their expertise in another approach to therapy. Thus, it is clear that subgroup identification (administrator; clinician) may affect these workers' reactions to change. However, employees thought to be most vulnerable to extreme stress are those who have little psychological connection to any group within the organization (that is, individuals with low levels of social identification).

These workers may find themselves isolated, unsupported, and at high risk of burnout (Haslam, O'Brien, Jetten, Vormedal, & Penna, 2005; O'Brien & Haslam, 2003). This hazard may befall social work students, particularly if they are the only intern assigned to their placement setting. It is important that supervisors minimize this risk by creating opportunities for these students to build connections with their coworkers within the organization.

A variety of demographic factors have also been examined in relation to workplace stress. Age appears to be correlated with burnout: Younger workers report higher levels of stress than do older ones (Maslach, 2005). Gender has also been found to influence the stress process. According to Cocchiara and Bell (2009), women experience certain unique employment-based stressors to a greater extent than do their male counterparts: lack of career progress, discrimination, stereotyping, and *interrole conflict* (conflicting expectations between their roles as employee and primary caretaker for their families). Other research has shown that, in response to threat, the female body produces hormones that trigger caregiving behavior (Taylor et al, 2000). Thus, when stressed, women are less inclined than are men to engage in fight or flight behavior and more inclined to search for comfort through interpersonal bonds and connections (that is, they "tend-and-befriend"). Members of oppressed groups might also be subject to higher degrees of occupational stress than are others. They have been found to experience stress that is additive to the general stressors that are experienced by all (Meyer, 2003). The dual perspective theory provides insight as to the nature of the stress process for cultural groups outside of the majority population (Norton, 1978). It suggests that every individual is a part of two surrounding systems: the nurturing system that is composed of family, friends, and other close associates and the sustaining environment that is made up of people in the wider community (including those in work settings). Conflict and strain result when the values, attitudes, and behaviors of the nurturing environment are incongruent with those of the sustaining environment. This lack of congruence and resulting strain is common for members of oppressed groups. By assuming a dual perspective, we appreciate the unique challenges that these workers face in adapting to the culture of their organization.

Finally, an individual's life experiences can contribute to the rise of stress-related difficulties on the job. For instance, a social worker's personal trauma history may increase his or her vulnerability to secondary traumatic stress (Figley, 1995) and vicarious trauma (Pearlman & Saakvitne, 1995). This is the likely result when indirect exposure to a client's trauma material

From the Field: Culture Clash

At the age of twenty-four, I began a graduate program in social work. I was drawn to the profession because of its focus on social change and on advocating for oppressed groups. I now see that I had an idolized view of the field and had disregarded how my own identity as a queer might clash with the culture of other social workers. My first wake-up call occurred at an orientation for students and their field instructors. It took place at the university and no requirements were set for attire. I came dressed in my usual gender queer clothing, which typically consists of nicely ironed male button down dress shirts and dress shorts or pants.

I met my agency field instructor who attended the orientation with another social worker who was employed at agency where I would be placed. My field instructor introduced me to this other worker who was a very gender normative female practitioner. I will never forget the look on her face when she turned to me. She appeared uncomfortable, hesitant, and disgusted by what she saw. At the end of our short conversation about the agency, she looked at me, pointed at my body from my head to my toes and stated, "You're going to have to step it up a bit." I recall immediately looking around and seeing my classmates dressed in sweat pants, t-shirts, and flip flop sandals. I was shocked. I was anxious about having to work with a person who immediately upon meeting me had a problem with my identity. I just wanted to cry. It was the second day of a two-year program and I already felt unwelcome.

When my internship began, my field instructor and other social workers at the agency attempted to make me feel welcome. Yet I could still feel the discomfort and stress regarding my experience with that social worker at the orientation. During supervision with my field instructor, I decided to share my experience. She advised me to limit my contact with that person and to inform her if any other incidents occurred. As the school year passed, other incidents did occur in which I questioned the intentions of this social worker. One day, she decided to apologize. She asked me to come inside her office and shut the door. Her apology consisted of "I just wanted to tell you that I am not homophobic." This comment made me feel even worse. Eventually, I shared my experiences with the director of the social work program. I was offered an opportunity to change my field placement, but I turned it down. I was not going to let that offensive person take away my opportunity to learn public adoption practice.

I share my experience today because often in our profession we are taught a concept known as "self-care." Literature and discussions of this topic often fail to acknowledge stressors on the practitioner, other than countertransference and secondary trauma. Years later, I can still clearly identify the stress, discomfort, and self-doubt I felt throughout that school year as a result of discrimination. However, through this experience I have come to realize that, as members of oppressed groups, we cannot control the hate or fear that others direct our way. We can only change ourselves. Self-care to me means finding a way to be at peace with oneself.

—*MJ*

triggerrs the worker's own unresolved traumatic conflicts. For this reason, it is important that trauma survivors avoid the temptation to "work on their own healing by helping others work through theirs" (Yassen, 1995, p. 196). It is recommended that these aspiring social workers and trauma survivors complete their own recovery process and allow for some space, time, and distance from their own experiences prior to taking on work responsibilities that involve close contact with client trauma.

Organizational Sources of Stress

Sources of stress go well beyond the personal, however, as has been demonstrated in a wide body of research on organizational factors that contribute to stress related conditions in employees. Most notably, a large-scale study ($N = 10,308$) was conducted with civil servants who worked in London between the years 1985 and 2000 (Kuper, Marmot, & Yamase, 2003). This research examined the relationships between various aspects of job strain and incidents of health-related problems. Results showed that *high job demands* (the requirement to work hard and quickly) and low *decision latitude* (lack of control over duties, timelines, and organizational decisions) were associated with an increased risk of coronary heart disease (CHD). In addition, high effort combined with low rewards was related to increased incidents of CHD and poor physical and mental functioning (Kuper, Singh-Manoux, Siegrist, & Marmot, 2002), whereas perceptions of injustice on the job were linked to absences from work because of illness (Head et al., 2007). *Justice climate* is a term that has been used in referring to worker perceptions regarding the level of fairness within their agency, especially as it relates to processes and procedures, interactions between supervisors and subordinates, and outcomes received by individuals. In general, unfavorable perceptions of justice within the organization have been associated with job strain (Elovainio, Kivimaki, & Helkama, 2001). Other work has identified *rank*, or position in the organization's hierarchy, as a determinant of stress. For example, Morin (2002) found a significant relationship between low perceived rank and increased vulnerability to the effects of occupational stress. Furthermore, Collins (2006) showed that when rank or status dynamics are not understood and processed, the result can be "defiant, deferential, or defensive behaviors on the part of the lower ranked employees" (p. 314). Therefore, it is important that organizational leaders do not underestimate the effects of their behavior toward subordinates (Offerman & Hellmann,

1996). Social work supervisors, in particular, need to be aware of the power they hold in the supervisory relationship and take responsibility for when, how, and why they choose to exercise it (Cousins, 2004).

Role conflict and role ambiguity have been identified as organizational sources of stress that are particularly relevant to social work. *Role conflict* occurs when employees are expected to carry out activities that are incongruent with their professional identity and training. This conflict may arise when the employee's role in the agency demands that they behave in a manner that is inconsistent with their values or provides limited opportunities for them to use their skills or knowledge. When there is a lack of clarity regarding work responsibilities, *role ambiguity* is the result. In a study of 259 mental health service providers, Acker (2003) found that both role conflict and ambiguity were significantly associated with two key dimensions of burnout: *emotional exhaustion* (feeling overextended and fatigued by one's work) and *depersonalization* (impersonal and detached responses toward clients). We recommend that organizations develop plans for combating burnout that involve increasing workers' satisfaction with their jobs.

The concept of *emotional labor* sheds light on an additional source of stress in social work. This type of labor requires the employee to regulate the expression of his or her emotions according to strong display rules. Workers who have customer or client contact are subject to the strongest pressures in this regard. When there is chronic disequilibrium between the worker's felt emotions and those he or she must exhibit, negative health and mental health consequences could result (Schaubroeck & Jones, 2000). As applied to social work, employees who have frequent contact with angry, hostile, or involuntary clients may be at highest risk for stress reactions of this kind. They may frequently find themselves in situations in which they are expected to mask their emotions when clients trigger their anger, anxiety, or fear. Two types of acting have been identified that are used by employees to help them comply with display rules: surface acting in which one modifies facial expression or body language and deep acting in which one alters his or her inner feelings. Research has shown that surface acting, unlike deep acting, is associated with higher levels of emotional exhaustion on the job (Grandey, 2003). This finding suggests that to limit the negative consequences of emotional labor, strategies are needed that not only help social workers manage their inner feelings, but also support their physical and emotional safety on the job.

Discrimination at the organizational and interactional level also contributes to high levels of workplace stress. Gaps in pay and limited access to promotions negatively affect white women, as well those of color, working in human service organizations (Weinbach, 2008). Cases concerning inequalities in hiring and firing practices on the basis of race, gender, age, class, religion, and sexual orientation appear in all sectors of the job market. On an interpersonal level, negative stereotypes of social workers that are based on demographic characteristics or professional roles result in misunderstanding and conflict on the job. When harassment occurs, the consequences can be dire. Ethnic harassment, gender harassment, and generalized workplace harassment predict a variety of strain outcomes, including low organizational commitment, poor job satisfaction, turnover intention, poor psychological well-being, and physical health problems (Raver & Nishii, 2010).

Finally, when the culture of an organization is toxic, stress reactions in employees are likely to occur. The *toxic culture* can be described as one in which workers are uncivil and uncooperative, human needs of individuals are ignored, and mistakes or discrepant views are not tolerated (Barnes, 2006). It is also one in which there is a lack of sensitivity toward others and "the name of the game is surviving, prospering, and acquiring control" (Frost, 2003, p. 57). For social workers, in particular, it can be demoralizing when their agency promotes what Morrison (1990) called *survival messages,* such as "don't feel, be strong, and don't admit mistakes" (p. 255). Such messages discount and devalue natural human emotions and assume that they indicate weakness or incompetence in the employee.

Bullying is a workplace stressor that often emerges within toxic cultures that lack effective supervision and leadership. It is a relatively common form of psychological aggression that can have serious adverse psychological and psychosomatic effects on its victims. Workplace bullying involves employee behaviors that are regular, repeated, and persistent and include harassing, offending, or socially excluding a coworker, threatening his or her status as a professional, or deliberately interfering with his or her work tasks (Einarsen, Hoel, Zapf, & Cooper, 2003). Organizational factors thought to contribute to bullying behavior include low psychosocial safety, perceived power imbalances, low perceived costs for perpetrators, low job satisfaction, and high internal competition (Bond, Tuckey, & Dollard, 2010).

To better understand this phenomenon as it applies to social work, van Heugten (2010) interviewed victims of bullying about their experiences. Frontline social workers relayed incidents in which their managers made harsh demands, yelled and swore at them, and called them names. They also described situations in which their supervisors probed into their personal

From the Field: Being Bullied

I was excited to start my first day of employment in a child welfare agency, having only graduated with my master's degree in social work three months previously. When I arrived at the agency, my supervisor asked that I spend the first week shadowing other social workers. I asked around, but it was difficult finding anyone willing to take me out into the field. When someone finally agreed, I was thrilled. Beth, a "seasoned" worker of four years, managed a caseload similar to the one I would be managing. It seemed a great first-day match. We visited a couple of homes and met with families. Then we headed out into a very rural, isolated area. It had been snowing and the weather was cold. The roads were slippery. Beth slowed the car and stopped on the side of the road. She turned to me and said, "You know that everyone in the office hates you, right?" I didn't know what to say. I nodded my head apprehensively. Beth continued, "You come in here with some degree, get more money than the rest of us, and it isn't fair." I stopped nodding. She finished, "You probably should watch your back, because there are a lot of angry social workers." She laughed. Loud. She then turned toward the steering wheel, started the car again, and drove to our last home visit.

I soon discovered that Beth was right, others were angry. On my fourth day on the job, my supervisor asked me to take on a case of my own. In preparation, I gathered a notepad, pencil, and bottle of water. Within minutes, Jen, an investigating social worker of over seven years, pointed at me from the end of the office cubicles and loudly stated, "You, MSW, let's go." I stood immediately and followed her, barely understanding what she was saying. "I told them not to give the case to a green worker but no one cares what I say." It became clear that conversations about me had occurred behind my back. I tried to respond, but she was walking so far in front of me, walking briskly, that I could not project loud enough for her to hear me. When we reached my supervisor's office, Jen said, "Here she is. Now what?" Jen, my supervisor, and I staffed my new case for nearly an hour. It was a difficult one. I drew a rough genogram and mapped family history and issues. I had notes on each parent, child, and extended family member known to the agency. I also made a "to do" list, with some comments about overdue referrals, missing placement paperwork, and lost child medication requests. I was looking at a tremendous amount of information and follow-up. After the staffing, I left my notes and the bottle of water at my desk, and went to the mailroom to find the needed forms to begin my work. When I returned, I passed Jen in the hall, and thanked her for the wealth of information she was able to provide about the family. She barely stopped, and mumbled as she left, "You're never going to get up to speed on this case."

(continued)

From the Field: Being Bullied *(continued)*

When I returned to my desk, my water bottle had been moved off of my notepad and my notes were gone. I searched my trash, empty drawers, and supervisor's office. I searched for over 30 minutes. When I finally saw Jen again, I asked if she had seen them. She stated, "Don't they teach you MSWs how to work a case without notes? Sounds like you are going to have to try. I told you that you were never going to be able to get up to speed." That was it. She walked away and I was left knowing that my notes were nowhere to be found.

This kind of treatment continued for nearly six months, in varying degrees of intensity. Sometimes it was in the form of a joke or sarcastic comment. Other times, my peers referred to me in their complaints to supervisors—as an example of how wages, caseload sizes, and case assignments were unfair. But worst of all was the purposeful disrespect, such as mean and spiteful remarks or discussions about me behind my back when I could clearly hear. I had not expected this aspect of my employment. And I had certainly not anticipated how it would impact my day-to-day work.

—*MLK*

histories and used information gathered to suggest the presence of a mental disorder or problems with authority. Supervisors themselves indicated that they were held to workload expectations that were excessive and unrewarded, and some suggested that difficult employees and clients were intentionally transferred to their teams. All stated that the bullying behavior lasted close to or longer than six months; some reported that it lasted two years or more.

Reader Reflections

1) How would you react if you were being bullied in your workplace?
2) What would you do if you saw a coworker being bullied?
3) What support would you need to address a problem with bullying in your agency?

To minimize workplace bullying and other forms of toxicity, administrators need to promote a value of compassion within their organization. Frost (2003) described the compassionate organization as one in which the emotional health of employees is valued, promoted, and preserved. It is also one where workers are hired and promoted for both attitude and skill. Finally, it is a setting in which supervisors "go beyond task-focused leadership" by validating their employees and taking the time to recognize and appreciate their efforts (Frost, 2003, p. 29).

Conclusion

For social workers striving to overcome the professional challenges they face, a thorough understanding of the stress process is vital. The literature across disciplines, including biology, medicine, sociology, clinical psychology, and organizational psychology, extensively explores this topic and offers useful information. The person-in-environment framework that forms the cornerstone for social work practice reveals that sources of stress can be found at both personal and organizational levels. Thus, responsibility for the management of stress in social work lies not only with agency supervisors and administrators, but also with individual employees. We call for a mutual commitment to the creation of compassionate organizations that support the self-care of all who dedicate their time and energy to this emotionally trying and taxing occupation.

Discussion Questions

1. Explain the similarities and differences between burnout, secondary traumatic stress, and vicarious trauma. Give an example of each.
2. Why might younger social workers be more vulnerable to burnout than older ones?
3. What could social work agencies do to respond to the "tend-and-befriend" tendency that might be present in female employees?
4. Why is it important for trauma survivors to complete their own recovery process prior to serving in a helping capacity with victims of trauma?
5. What can be done to transform a toxic organizational culture?

Chapter Exercises

1. Social Identity

Each person has one or more social identities as it relates to their work environment.

How would you describe yours?

Over the upcoming week, take notice of the people in your agency, those who have a social identity that is similar to yours and those who are different.

What issues seem important to employees across groups?

Are the issues similar or different? What appears to trigger stress for people who share your social identity?

2. Emotional Labor

Reflect on an occasion on the job when you masked your emotions while in communication with a client.

What were your true feelings and what prompted them?

What emotions did you project instead?

What were the display rules that guided your cover-up?

Did you engage in surface acting?

What would deep acting have involved?

3. Compassionate Organization

Imagine that you are entering the main office of a compassionate social work organization.

What is the first thing you notice?

As you travel through the work setting, what more do you observe about the way employees and supervisors behave? Give specific examples.

Now, consider and describe ways that you can bring more compassion to your organization.

Chapter 2
Self-Care as a Solution

Visualize yourself as social worker who is displaying signs of chronic stress. You are tired, seem unmotivated to complete your assigned duties, and are avoiding contact with certain clients and colleagues. Your supervisor becomes concerned and urges you to practice better self-care. Imagine how you might respond. Would you feel supported? Would you be clear about how to interpret this recommendation? What would you understand better self-care to mean? If you are like many workers in the field, this feedback might be quite confusing. It might even feel more like an admonishment and less like an indication of genuine care and concern. Nevertheless, you might take the comment to heart and attempt to make improvements in your lifestyle or in your time management on the job. Yet, you might not see any lasting change in your level of stress and strain in the workplace.

The scenario described above is increasingly common, particularly because the notion of self-care has become popular in the field of social work. With good intentions, many social work educators, supervisors, and managers are now encouraging it as a means of sustaining student interns and employees through difficult times. Yet, often those making this suggestion have little to offer in the way of an in-depth explanation of what self-care really means. To meet the need for a more robust understanding of the term, we have conducted focus groups with social work practitioners described in the chapters to follow. In this chapter, we provide an overview of the literature that shows how the concept has evolved in recent years across disciplines. We also share types of self-care—practices that typically concern lifestyle and/or workplace adjustments—recommended by experts on burnout and secondary trauma.

What is Self-Care?

Definitions of *self-care* vary to some extent across different helping professions. One study that examined the term found 139 definitions in the literature across disciplines (Godfrey, et al., 2011). These varied definitions, however, share certain characteristics. One commonality is the focus on *deprofessionalized care*, meaning that patients, clients, or consumers take a more active role in their own care versus relying strictly on professionals to provide healing. Gantz (1990) reviewed definitions from six different disciplines: medicine, nursing, health education, psychology, sociology, and public health. She noted that across these fields "The concept [of self-care]

- is situation and culture specific;
- involves the capacity to act and to make choices;
- is influenced by knowledge, skills, values, locus of control, and efficacy; and
- focuses on aspects of health care under individual control (as opposed to social policy or legislation)." (Gantz, 1990, p. 2)

The literature also specifies some unique aspects of self-care found within various professions. For example, the promotion of self-care among physicians entails a transfer of responsibility for certain aspects of care from doctor to patient (Gantz, 1990). It involves the patient taking on a set of activities at the direction of a physician or other health care provider to prevent or alleviate symptoms or deal with a specific medical problem. In the medical field, there is not a general agreement about whether self-care refers to restoring health, promoting health, preventing illness, or possibly all three. The medical literature does discuss patient self-care after all types of surgery and for people with many types of illnesses. For example, researchers and medical practitioners discuss this concept as it relates to people who have diabetes. Self-care in this case would require that patients monitor their blood sugar and eat appropriately for the condition. Another example involves patients controlling their asthma by reducing exposure to things that can trigger asthma attacks and preventatively taking medication. According to medical experts, self-care requires that individuals accurately assess their risk and take appropriate steps to improve their health, while decreasing the need for physician visits.

In nursing, self-care is defined a bit more broadly. Here it concerns a patient's ability to engage in "healthy lifestyle behavior required for human development and functioning, as well as those activities required to manage acute and chronic healthcare conditions" (Richard & Shea, 2011, p. 256). Demands for self-care are said to include those that are universal and developmental and those made by health deviations (McCormack, 2003). Universal self-care is required by all human beings to meet basic needs for food, water, nurturing, and so on. Developmental self-care is needed for successful adaptation to various lifespan events or needs. Alternately, self-care devoted to health deviation is focused on coping with illness or injury experiences. The *self-care deficit* is the focus of some researchers and practitioners in the nursing field. This deficit occurs when patients' therapeutic demands exceed their capability to perform self-care activities (Orem, 1995; White, Peters, & Schim, 2011). Others emphasize a holistic and collaborative approach to nursing in which the expectations of the patient and his or her family members are determined and a plan of self-care is created that matches patient choice and receptivity (Furlong, 1996). The focus is on developing a partnership with patients to enhance their degree of involvement in their own care.

Traditional work in the field of psychology examines self-care through its various psychological components, including self-concept, confidence, efficacy, esteem, and health-related beliefs and perceptions. Barofsky (1987) focused on self-care as it relates to patient compliance with medical treatment recommendations. He viewed it as a form of self-control and as an important outcome of any therapeutic process. Others have advanced the health belief model (HBM) that attempts to explain health-oriented behavior. This model assumes that individuals will take health-promoting action when they believe that they are at risk of developing a serious and harmful condition, they expect that the recommended action will enable them to avoid the condition, and they believe they can be successful in taking this action (Glanz, 2005). HBM has been applied to preventative health behaviors and compliance with treatment regimes. Psychological studies also show that individuals' level of self-worth influences how well they care for themselves. For example, Chamberlain and colleagues (2007) found that a woman's perception of herself as worthy of care is related to whether or not she is likely to access needed medical services. Other research suggests that children's sense of self-worth and perceived social acceptance are linked to how well they care for themselves (Primeau & Ferguson, 1999).

These concepts and definitions are useful when our interest is in helping clients or consumers manage health conditions or improve their physiological functioning. However, for the purpose of this book, we are more interested in examining self-care as it relates to those who provide rather than receive services. This orientation focuses on the actions a helping professional takes "to lessen the amount of stress, anxiety, or emotional reaction experienced when working with clients" (Williams et al., 2010, p. 322). Even more broadly, self-care is a process through which deliberate choices are made about how to respond mentally, emotionally, and behaviorally to a variety of work-related stressors. It is also viewed as a movement toward the adoption of perspectives and practices into the social worker's life that are intended to improve mental and physical health and well-being and to reduce or prevent various types of stress-related conditions. In a social service or social change environment, self-care is about learning to love, accept, and nurture oneself as a precursor to taking care of others.

Previous work done in the field of psychology on stress and coping is particularly applicable to self-care in the helping professions. Lazarus and Folkman (1984) distinguished between two primary types of coping: problem-focused and emotion-focused. *Problem-focused coping* is devoted to changing the circumstances that trigger our stress. For example, if an individual is stressed because his or her supervisor is angry and argumentative, problem-focused coping might involve requesting a transfer into another program or to a different supervisor. When such problem-solving efforts are out of reach or unsuccessful, *emotion-focused coping* is needed. This involves managing our emotional responses to the stressor by obtaining support or engaging in distracting activities. Examples of emotion-focused coping might include talking to friends about a stressful situation or going for a walk when the stress intensifies. Others have classified coping responses as active-cognitive coping, active-behavioral coping (Lazarus, 1966; Moos, 1977), or avoidance coping (Billings & Moos, 1981). *Active-cognitive coping* entails altering our view of the problem situation so that it appears more manageable; *active-behavioral coping* involves overt attempts to deal directly with a problem and its effects. In contrast, *avoidance coping* is focused on avoiding situations that would require us to actively confront a problem. It also involves efforts to reduce the emotional tension produced by the stressful situation through such behavior as sleeping, smoking, or drinking alcohol. According to Folkman and Moskowitz (2004), such escapist forms of coping are consistently linked with poor mental health outcomes. They recommended the use of future-oriented, or *proactive coping,* as a means of preventing or muting the adverse effects of potential stressors. Aspinwall and Taylor (1997) specified five elements of this form of coping: building a reserve of resources,

Types of Coping Responses

Problem	Active-Behavioral Coping	Active-Cognitive Coping	Avoidance Coping	Proactive Coping
You have missed a deadline on an assigned report.	You request an extension on the report due date and rearrange your schedule to complete the assignment.	You acknowledge time management as a challenge to be overcome.	You take a sick day when you are not sick to avoid the supervisor who has asked to speak with you about this problem.	You pre-plan your schedule to ensure time for completion of assigned reports.
A client has complained to your supervisor about services you provided.	You openly discuss these issues with your client to remedy the focus of complaints, as appropriate.	You recognize the value of client feedback in contributing to your professional growth.	You avoid or refuse contact with the client who has made the complaint.	You solicit feedback from your clients and process any concerns before they rise to the level of complaint.
A colleague has commented that you have "screwed up" a case that she transferred to you.	You ask this colleague for feedback on what they would like to see happen in this case. You nondefensively share your experience since taking over.	You recognize the importance of good communication with your coworkers AND that you can't control other people's behavior.	You avoid contact with this colleague and let other coworkers know that you are upset about this comment.	You obtain all information needed to be as successful as possible in taking on new case. You do your part in maintaining good coworker relationships.

identifying potential stressors and initial appraisal of these events, beginning coping efforts, and using feedback about the success of these efforts.
Proactive coping may be particularly beneficial for social work practitioners
in so far as it guides them to anticipate difficult encounters, consider their
appraisal of the stressors they will face, and plan a course of action accordingly. This type of coping response is discussed in greater depth in chapter 7.

Reader Reflections

On the basis of your review of various types of coping responses shown in *Types of
Coping Responses,* answer the following:

1) In what situations have you used active-behavioral coping? What were the
   results?
2) When have you used active-cognitive coping? Was this coping effort helpful?
   If so, how?
3) When have you used avoidant coping? Was this coping response helpful?
   Might active coping have produced a different outcome?

History of Self-Care

According to Kickbusch (1989), academics of the late 1970s "discovered"
that people take care of themselves and they began to label this behavior
self-care. She likened this revelation to the academic discovery of poverty in
the 1960s. Clearly, both self-care and poverty had long been occurring, but
they were not previously seen as worthy of note or study. Once self-care was
recognized, the concept began to flourish. In fact, the notion of taking care
of oneself, rather than relying on expert outsiders, was a central theme of the
women's movement in the 1970s. The philosophy of feminism asserted that
women should have control over their bodies, reproductive choices, and the
opportunity to be informed decision makers in their gynecological care. This
movement may have, in fact, been one of the driving forces that launched the
notion of self-care into the public sphere. The growing interest in self-care
also coincided with the growth of the self-help movement that focused on the
use of publicly available information and group support to assist individuals
recovering from a psychological or substance abuse disorder. Both were in
part a reaction to the increasing "medicalization" of what were otherwise
seen as nonmedical facets of people's lives (Schiller & Levin, 1983). The
empowerment perspective advanced in the mental health field in the 1990s

What Self-Care Is Not

- It is NOT only for burned out workers
- It is NOT only for the weak and maladjusted
- It is NOT something that we don't have time to do
- It is NOT about focusing on self to the exclusion of others
- It is NOT about numbing ourselves from discomfort
- It is NOT an indication of narcissism
- It is NOT an unjustifiable luxury
- It is NOT about self-indulgence

furthered understanding of self-guided care. It emphasized the importance of a service delivery process that builds on the expertise of clients and consumers, while providing them with choice, decision-making power, and access to needed resources.

The concept of *self-care* as an antidote to various types of stress experienced by human service providers is, for the most part, a 21st-century phenomenon. In a 2002 publication, Gentry defined it as the "ability to refill and refuel oneself in healthy ways" and stressed its value in the prevention of compassion fatigue in those who treat trauma survivors (p. 48). He portrayed the self-care plan as an important protective device that is akin to that of the seatbelt for the driver behind the wheel of an automobile. Similarly, Kearney, Weininger, Vachon, Harrison, and Mount (2009) argued that self-care is essential to the therapeutic mandate, as it allows practitioners to provide care "in a sustainable way with greater compassion, sensitivity, effectiveness, and empathy (p. 1157)." In support of this view, they aptly quoted, "The heart must first pump blood to itself" (Shapiro, 2008, as cited in Kearney, 2009, p. 1162). Finally, Norcross and Guy (2007) referred to self-care as an ethical imperative for mental health practitioners, including social workers. In fact, various behavioral health professional associations clarify its importance in the code of conduct specific to their profession. The NASW (2008) *Code of Ethics* asserts that it is the responsibility of the social worker to address any serious need for self-care in his or her colleagues. When a social worker has knowledge of a coworker's impairment resulting from psychological distress that is interfering with his or her practice effectiveness, the social worker is advised to consult with that colleague and assist him or her in "taking remedial action" (NASW, 2008).

Research on Self-Care

Very little research has been conducted on self-care in the helping professions. However, a few studies have linked various aspects of self-care to enhanced coping in human service providers. In a review of several of these studies, Pearlman (1999) learned that participating in leisure activities, taking a vacation, or socializing with friends or family are strategies reported to be particularly helpful to psychologists and other mental health workers in managing the stresses of their work. Similarly, an exploratory study conducted by Turner and colleagues (2005) revealed that the most effective self-care activities for psychology interns involved family and friend support, pleasurable experiences, and humor. On the basis of interviews with clinicians working with trauma survivors, Killian (2008) found the following to be beneficial to them in preventing compassion fatigue and burnout: having a reasonably sized caseload, having regular supervision and a supportive work environment, processing with peers, having a social network, being optimistic, and developing self-awareness. A study by Alkema, Linton, and Davis (2008) examined the relationship between self-care and levels of compassion fatigue, burnout, and compassion satisfaction in hospice professionals. Data were collected from 35 workers by using the Professional Quality of Life Instrument (Stamm, 2002) and the Self-Care Assessment Worksheet (Saakvitne & Pearlman, 1996). The latter assesses, by self-report, the frequency of activities performed by workers within the following areas:

- *physical self-care* (eating well, exercising, sleeping adequately, getting massages, accessing medical care, etc.),
- *psychological self-care* (self-reflecting, engaging in leisure activities, journaling, practicing receiving from others, etc.),
- *emotional self-care* (praising oneself, engaging in laughter/play, expressing outrage through appropriate channels, etc.),
- *spiritual self-care* (praying, meditating, developing awareness of nonmaterial aspects of life, etc.),
- *professional self-care* (taking a break, making quiet time, balancing caseload, arranging work space, etc.), and
- *balance* (among work, family, relationships, play, rest, etc.).

Results showed that the workers who take part in a variety of these self-care activities were less likely to report high levels of burnout or compassion fatigue. Furthermore, the use of emotional and spiritual forms of self-care were related to higher levels of *compassion satisfaction*, defined as the pleasure derived from being helpful to others.

A recent qualitative study also sheds some light on the value in several innovative self-care strategies: mindfulness, self-hypnosis, music, and spirituality (Williams, Richardson, Moore, Eubanks Gamble, & Keeling, 2010). Four mental health therapists committed to the use of one of these methods over a 2-week period. They each provided an in-depth written account of the effect of their self-care practice on their personal life and interactions with clients. Their reflections reveal that all of these methods were beneficial. They helped the therapists manage stress and anxiety, create balance in their lives, and view their clients with compassion.

Reader Reflections

1) Which of the struggles with self-care noted in Struggles with Self-Care (see p. 34) do you most identify with?
2) What support do you need to overcome your challenges in maintaining a consistent approach to self-care?
3) Which of the activities listed in What Does Self-Care Mean to You? (see p. 35) might you incorporate into your daily or weekly routine?
4) Are there activities not mentioned that you could add to the list?
5) What strengths do you have that help you implement self-care strategies?

Types of Self-Care

Authors in the field of social work and related disciplines have advocated a variety of approaches to self-care. These generally fall into one of two main categories: *lifestyle choices* and *workplace adaptations*. First, numerous behaviors related to lifestyle have been recommended to human service professionals seeking to manage their stress. For example, the maintenance of a healthy diet is widely discussed as an important self-care strategy. In fact, there is ample evidence showing that good nutrition improves levels of cholesterol, as well as blood pressure, thereby exerting a strong protective effect on health (Harvard Health Publications, 2010). Research also indicates that stress raises metabolism and depletes the body of various vitamins and minerals (Takeda et al., 2004). Thus, it is especially important that highly stressed social workers eat well to replace these depleted nutrients. Hays (1999) further recommended that practitioners establish a steady rhythm

Struggles with Self-Care

When asked to discuss their challenges with self-care, MSW students offered the comments below:

"The majority of the time I feel as if self-care and time management are interlocked and inseparable. This year has been extremely busy and I am often so wrapped up in the state of mind that I need to work, work, work to get things done that I don't allow myself to breathe or do something enjoyable."

"I attempt to keep a balanced diet and exercise, but this aspect of self-care is seriously lacking for me. At this point, I am trying to find a balance to achieve this. I also get only minimal to moderate amounts of sleep on a regular basis. It is difficult for me to get enough rest because I have excessive amounts of work to accomplish at home."

"The society in which I reside doesn't seem to value self-care—which makes it difficult to take time to appropriately care for myself. That's why I often become extremely frustrated and grumpy!"

"When my job is overwhelming, I forget to take care of myself and dedicate all of my time and energy to work."

"The difficulty with self-care is that most people see it as concept and don't take action and incorporate it into their life."

of blood glucose and a consistent routine for eating. Following a regular exercise routine that includes aerobic and anaerobic activities is also strongly encouraged for professional caregivers (Gentry, 2008). Exercise reduces the risk of certain medical disorders and has preventative and therapeutic psychological benefits (Walsh, 2011). It releases endorphins in the body that enhance our mood and well-being. In addition, research shows that exercise has a positive effect on self-esteem and self-worth, thus increasing the likelihood of continued engagement in self-care (Elavsky, 2010; Stathopoulou et al., 2006). Preserving time for adequate sleep is also known to be very important. Insufficient sleep can increase the risk of a number of adverse medical conditions, including diabetes, high blood pressure, hypertension, and memory loss (Knutson, Spiegel, Peneva, & Cautera, 2007). It can also result in mood disturbances and distressing emotions such as anger and anxiety (National Sleep Foundation, 2006). Skovholt and Trotter-Mathison (2011) suggested that practitioners in the caring professions use several techniques for promoting good *sleep hygiene*: going to bed at the same time each night and waking at the same time each morning, developing an evening routine

What Does Self-Care Mean to You?

When asked to comment on what comes to mind when they think of self-care, social workers and students generated the following list of activities:

- Going on a silent retreat
- Getting away from your normal routine
- Weekend hikes
- A little shopping
- Having fun
- Being out in nature
- Laughing
- Eating healthy food
- Spoiling yourself with chocolate
- Say "no" at times
- Going to the gym
- Sleeping in
- Taking a long shower
- Getting a massage or facial
- Gardening
- Going to church/temple
- Getting help from coworkers
- Bringing your true feelings to supervision
- Taking lunch breaks consistently
- Reading a book, watching a movie
- Spend time with friends and family
- Taking a walk
- Grocery shopping and cooking
- Re-arranging your furniture
- Chopping wood
- Lifting weights
- Writing

that promotes relaxation, and avoiding the use of the bedroom for work or watching television.

Social self-care is also recognized as vital to the high-functioning social worker. This amounts to "having a life outside of work that involves doing what the practitioner enjoys and spending time with family and friends" (Pryce et al., 2007, p. 62). Positive relationships, in particular, have been linked to health and happiness (Fowler & Christakis, 2009; Jetten, Haslam, Haslam, & Branscombe, 2009) and the prevention of compassion fatigue

Chopra's Suggestions for Healthy Eating

Medical doctor, spiritual leader, and best-selling author, Deepak Chopra (2002) asserts that good food can be one of the best medicines we have at our disposal. He encourages us to listen to our bodies and what they tell us about the food we need in order to function optimally. Dr. Chopra states that there are six basic tastes that should be covered in our diet, if we are to avoid chemical imbalance and addictive cravings. They are as follows:

- *Sweet:* Foods that have a sweet flavor increase body bulk. They include carbohydrates, protein, and fats, as provided by grains, nuts, fruits, starchy vegetables, and animal products. From this group, it is best to eat fresh fruits and vegetables, whole gains, and nuts, while avoiding red meat.
- *Sour:* Foods in this group are mildly acidic, such as grapefruits, berries and tomatoes. In addition to these fruits, small servings of low fat yogurt or feta cheese are recommended. Aged sour cheeses should be eaten in moderation, as they are high in cholesterol.
- *Salty:* This flavor is not only produced by table salt, but also soy sauce and tamari. In small amounts, salty foods aid in digestion, but too much can result in fluid retention and high blood pressure.
- *Pungent:* These flavors stimulate digestion and help mobilize stagnant secretions. Seasonings such as pepper and ginger contain natural antioxidants, while garlic may help to lower cholesterol.
- *Bitter:* Many green and yellow vegetables are bitter and contain detoxifying and disease-preventing properties. Cauliflower and broccoli may help prevent cancer and heart disease; green peppers, cabbage and asparagus help fight infections and may reduce risk of memory loss.
- *Astringent:* Foods such as beans, legumes, and peas fall into this flavor group and provide an excellent source of fiber and vegetable protein. Some fruits are astringent, such as cranberries and pomegranates. Green tea is astringent as well, and is believed to provide a good source of cancer preventing chemicals.

*Dr. Chopra also urges us to eat with awareness and use food to fill the emptiness in our stomach, not in our heart. He offers nutrition plans and recipes in his book *The Chopra Center Cookbook: Nourishing Body and Soul.*

in caregivers (Gentry, 2008). According to Walsh (2011), participation in relaxing, recreational, creative, or spiritually oriented activities enhances both physical and emotional health. He also stressed the importance of avoiding excessive media immersion, as the constant barrage of television and digital stimulation can exact a toll on us physically and psychologically.

The Benefits of Stretching

Stretching is a type of exercise in which specific muscles are elongated in a purposeful manner. It is designed primarily to increase muscle elasticity and tone. Internationally recognized sports injury consultant, Brad Walker (2011), stated that five additional benefits of stretching are:

- *Increased flexibility* (this reduces your risk of muscle strains or sprains)
- *Improved circulation* (this increases blood flow to the muscles and helps remove waste)
- *Improved balance and coordination* (this reduces your risk of falls)
- *Reduced back pain* (caused by stiff and tight muscles)
- *Improved cardiovascular health* (by lowering blood pressure and improves artery function)

Some stretching can easily be done in an office setting. For example, while seated, one can do shoulder shrugs, torso stretches, spinal twists, and forearm as well as neck stretches. For instructions on how to do these exercises properly, see Paige Waehner's Web page at: http://exercise.about.com/od/flexibility workouts/tp/officestretches.htm

Furthermore, when we spend a large amount of time with the simulated world portrayed by contemporary media, we become largely divorced from the natural world around us. Setting aside time to be in natural settings is recommended as a form of therapy that is highly restorative and has no known side effects. A final lifestyle choice that is often suggested involves establishing clear boundaries between work and home. In fact, striking a workable balance between our professional and personal lives is noted to be an essential aspect of self-care (Williams et al., 2010).

A number of workplace adaptations have also been suggested to social workers who are struggling with high levels of stress. For example, to alleviate symptoms of secondary trauma, child welfare workers are encouraged by Pryce and colleagues (2007) to "start the day with a list of work to be achieved, prioritize it, and then try to organize it so that emotionally draining tasks are not piled together" (p.64). They concurred with the recommendations of Saakvitne and Pearlman (1996) who focused on professional self-care in trauma therapists. Practitioners are urged to plan breaks in their work day, arrange their workspace so that it is comfortable and comforting, get up and move around, and have free weights at their desk that can be used to relieve pain and tension in the neck and back. It is also suggested that they identify and initiate projects that they can enjoy and find rewarding.

Experts in the field of burnout have discussed the benefits of making temporary changes in work, or "downshifts," to a less demanding task before returning to a challenging activity (Maslach & Leiter, 2005a). They have also asserted that we do not have to be "the lone person who does everything" in our agency; we must learn how to delegate tasks, train others to do them, and encourage coworker s to share responsibility (Maslach & Leiter, 2005a, p. 47). The importance of being assertive and clearly defining one's limits has also been emphasized. Prior to agreeing to taking on tasks that are not essential to their own areas of responsibility, workers are encouraged to say, "Let me think about it." This response affords them time to evaluate the pros

From the Field: Speaking Up

I was really excited to get a job working as a clinical social worker for a community-based mental health agency. It was what I always wanted to do. Everyone was very welcoming and I was happy to be there. My boss started giving me clients but said she wanted to start me out slow until I was oriented to the job. She also wanted me to translate for some of the other clinicians who had monolingual Spanish speaking families on their caseload. Oh, by the way, I am bi-lingual and knew that this gave me a boost up in terms of getting the job. I was proud to translate because I knew how hard it is for Spanish speaking families to feel comfortable getting therapy. But over time, I started to resent the constant requests for translation. This is not what I had trained to do! I also began to feel frustrated that the only clients that were being assigned to me were Spanish speaking ones. Don't get me wrong, I love working with these families, but I began to feel boxed in. I wanted some variety in my caseload. But I was afraid to say anything. I didn't want my supervisor to think that I was ungrateful for having the opportunity to work at the agency. I also didn't want to make her mad. So I kept my mouth shut. Eventually, I started to get stressed out and depressed. I went to see a counselor who helped my think about ways I could speak up more about my needs at work and with my family. Finally, I told my boss how I was feeling and she completely understood. She started assigning me families with different cultural backgrounds and it was really great. Since then I have been learning a lot about people of varying ethnicities. I also have learned how important it is to speak up and advocate for yourself on the job. You may not get what you want, but it can't hurt.

—Rosa

and cons of taking on an additional assignment (Pryce et al., 2007). Social workers may also benefit by becoming involved in agency-based discussions, focus groups, or committee work devoted to addressing caseload and workload issues. Furthermore, it is important that they develop the negotiation skills required to successfully advocate for their needs pertaining to case assignments, pay, benefits, and vacation. Another workplace recommendation focuses on the use of supervisory or peer support. Talking to a trusted supervisor or colleague about painful or challenging experiences is said to help human service workers de-stress (Barnes, 2006), feel connected, recognize their successes, identify solutions, and find humor in troubling events (Moran, 2002).

These strategies for advancing self-care through lifestyle and workplace adjustments are both well-reasoned and sensible. When implemented, they are likely to contribute to overall health and efficiency on the job. Yet, as seen in student comments noted in *Struggles with Self-Care,* they are sometimes difficult to sustain over the long haul. They fall short of clarifying processes for cognitive coping with the stressors typically encountered in social work and they fail to provide tools for enhancing the psychological safety within social service settings or for managing inconsistencies between the employee's work style and the culture of his or her organization. In the chapters to follow, we devote attention to these topics with the aim of expanding views of stress management in our profession.

Reader Reflections

1) What workplace adaptations might be helpful to you in coping with stress?
2) Are there times when you take on more work than you should?
3) Do you access peer and supervisory support, as needed?
4) In what areas would it be important for you to advocate for your needs?

Conclusion

Self-care is frequently prescribed as a cure for an assortment of stress-related conditions seen in helping professionals. It is also touted as a necessary prerequisite to service delivery that is compassionate, ethical, and effective. Yet, despite the increasing importance placed on self-care, its meaning has not been fully explored. Moreover, the process for achieving it has been only superficially addressed. What is clear is that the concept of self-care has been and continues to be evolving. Although many of the self-care strategies pre-viously advanced are valid and important to consider in approaching the management of stress in social work, they are not enough—but they do provide an important starting point for our journey into the deeper realms of self-care.

Discussion Questions

1. What is the difference between problem-focused and emotion-focused coping? Give an example of each from your own life. How might you use proactive coping to manage work-related stress?
2. Why is it an ethical imperative that social workers engage in self-care?
3. What are some things a social worker can do to achieve better balance between their professional and personal lives?
4. What lifestyle choices do you make that promote healthy functioning? What improvements could you make with respect to this type of self-care?
5. What workplace adjustments have you used successfully in managing stress?

Chapter Exercises

1. Misconceptions about Self-Care

Ask coworkers in your office to comment on their perceptions of self-care, including when and for whom it is needed. Notice any of their misconceptions, as countered in *What Self-Care Is Not.*

Have you shared any of these beliefs at any time in your career?

2. Making Time for Self-Care

Review your calendar and identify small amounts of time each week for a self-care activity that you know makes you feel relaxed, centered, and recharged. Record the activity on your calendar and make a deal with yourself that for one month you will not let anything get in the way of your completing this self-care task. At the conclusion of the month, observe any effects your efforts at self-care have had on your physical, emotional, or professional functioning.

Have you slept better? Felt calmer? Been less irritable? Been more energetic or efficient?

Also, honestly appraise any barriers that interfered with your commitment to self-care. Consider how you will deal with these barriers in the future.

3. Excessive Media Immersion

Reflect on the views of Walsh (2011) with regard to the effects of "excessive media immersion." He noted that in modern times we are flooded each day with multimedia stimuli, including those produced by television, computers, cell phones, and other electronic devices. Next, monitor the extent to which you are engaged in the multimedia world versus the natural world around you.

Are you excessively immersed in contemporary media? If so, does this result in any "techno-stress"?

What self-care solution can you bring to this challenge?

PART II
Personal Strategies for Self-Care

Chapter 3
Self-Awareness

Your vision will become clear only when you look into your heart. Who looks outside, dreams. Who looks inside, awakens.
—CARL JUNG

Such words may inspire some to travel into the realm of self-awareness and make a concerted effort to reflect on their own beliefs, attitudes, internal states, emotions, and traits. For many of us, however, this journey is quite rugged as we routinely run into a host of interferences, distractions, excuses, and tendencies to avoid our true feelings. Yet, if we venture forward, the benefits are bound to outweigh the hardships, particularly when our aim is to enhance our awareness of self as a social worker. This chapter is designed to facilitate the process of self-awareness in practitioners who encounter various forms of stress in their role as professional helper. We suggest that such awareness of self is a capacity that establishes the groundwork for self-care.

Spotting Signs of Stress

When asked to identify the signs and signals of stress overload that are rooted in their professional lives, the responses of social workers are enormously varied. Some indicate that, as a result of their demanding and emotionally taxing roles, they develop physical symptoms such as tension or pains in the head, neck, back, or stomach. Others admit that they grind their teeth, stutter and stammer, or experience tremors or twitches. A few note that they have panic attacks or heart palpitations, whereas others acknowledge becoming constipated or having bouts of diarrhea. Dr. Jennifer Ashton has reported

What Are Your Signs of Stress?

Review the following list of signs and symptoms of stress and identify those that you have experienced in recent weeks or months.

Physical Signs
- Headaches
- Tension or pain in neck, back, or stomach
- Digestion difficulties, constipation, diarrhea
- Stuttering or stammering
- Excessive sweating
- Tremors or twitches
- Heart palpitations, panic attacks
- Increased or decreased appetite
- Insomnia or hypersomnia
- Cravings for certain foods
- Skin conditions (acne, eczema, psoriasis)
- Dry mouth
- Hair loss

Mental Signs
- Poor concentration
- Forgetfulness
- Memory loss
- Lack of organization
- Confusion

on some less known bodily signs of stress (CBS News, 2010). She stated that stress has been found to trigger cravings for chocolate or carbohydrates (after all the word *stressed* is *desserts* spelled backwards!). In some cases, it is said to result in acne, eczema, psoriasis, and other skin conditions, worsened allergies, or even hair loss.

Symptoms of a mental or emotional nature are also quite common in individuals struggling with high levels of workplace stress. Many social workers report lapses in concentration or short-term memory when stressed. Others find themselves becoming disorganized, confused, and having difficulty making decisions. Some may even ruminate about minute details of their case-carrying responsibilities. Still others develop suspicious and hostile attitudes toward others or suffer from disturbing dreams and nightmares. Emotional

- Difficulty making decisions
- Rumination about details
- Suspicious or hostile attitudes
- Nightmares

Emotional Signs
- Anxious moods
- Depressed moods
- Angry moods
- Crying spells
- Excessive worrying
- Irrational fears
- Feelings of hopelessness
- Suicidal or homicidal thoughts

Behavioral Signs
- Irritability
- Impatience
- Defensiveness
- Blaming, judging others
- Social withdrawal
- Nervous habits
- Reduced motivation
- Increased use of alcohol, drugs

symptoms commonly reported as a result of excessive stress are crying spells, depressed or anxious moods, and even thoughts of death or suicide.

It is clear that our behavior can also be affected by occupational stress. After a particularly difficult and trying week on the job, we might notice that we are unusually impatient and irritable with our colleagues or our own friends and family members. We may have become defensive or blaming in our communication or have avoided interacting with others altogether. It is also possible that we have lost interest in our appearance or in performing to our ability. We may have developed nervous habits like fidgeting, tapping, and nail biting or dependencies on alcohol, nicotine, or prescription drugs.

Some mental, emotional, or behavioral signs of stress are related to our over-involvement or preoccupation with the clients we serve. In this case, we may leave the office, only to find ourselves worrying excessively about our clients' welfare. We may obsess about things we might have done differently to help them and ignore our friends and family members. Alternately, we might notice that we have become increasingly agitated and upset over circumstances in our own life that run parallel to those of clients we have seen in recent days or weeks. Quite unexpectedly, we may have memories or intrusive images of troubling events, either case-related or personal. Such experiences are not at all uncommon for practicing social workers.

Reader Reflections

On the basis of your review of the various signs of stress listed in *What Are Your Signs of Stress?,* answer the following:

1) How do you know when you are stressed? What are your earliest signs and
1) symptoms?
2) What tends to happen for you physically, emotionally, mentally, or behaviorally when you are experiencing stress overload?

The key to spotting signs of stress is noticing irregularities in our bodily functions, mental aptitudes and attitudes, moods and emotions, and in our behavior. However, when we engage in this form of self-monitoring, it is vitally important that we assume a nonjudgmental perspective. Instead of berating ourselves for succumbing to the stress involved in our profession, we might recognize instead that we have merely reached our limit. We can view the signs of stress as messengers, prompting us to "stop struggling and look directly at what is threatening us" (Chodron, 2002, p. 19). This encounter would undoubtedly bring us face to face with a variety of emotional reactions to various work-related circumstances. Ideally, it would result in an honest appraisal of our beliefs and perceptions about ourselves in relation to the work we do, the clients we serve, and the organizations of which we are a part. If we are willing to go down this road, we are truly on our way to self-care.

Examining Your Emotions

A central aspect of self-awareness concerns our ability to recognize and understand our emotions before they contribute to stress-related symptoms. This capacity is furthered when we practice tuning into our moment-to-moment emotional experience. Hence, we are likely to find that work-related situations stir within us an assortment of feelings. For instance, we may experience disappointment when a client relapses, fails to show for a scheduled appointment, or neglects to follow through with a planned intervention. Later, we may feel sadness and sympathy for a client who is in physical or psychological pain. Another time, we may discover that we are filled with apprehension and anxiety as we anticipate a meeting devoted to a review of our job performance. We may also feel anger when a client demonstrates an emergent need for services that are not available or affordable anywhere in the community. Conversely, we may experience a sense of pride and satisfaction when we receive recognition for a project well done.

In exploring our emotions, it is important to understand that they are neither good nor bad. In fact, all emotions, even the unpleasant ones, are actually clues to the truth about where we are vulnerable and what we value. For example, anxiety can be seen as a signal that we are moving into unknown territory. It can stimulate us to draw on our strengths so that we are able to preserve a sense of competence in the face of challenges. Similarly, frustration informs us that we have encountered a barrier toward a desired goal. In the best-case scenario, it prompts us to carefully consider the various options for going forward. Guilt notifies us that we have taken some action that runs counter to our prized values. Under the best of circumstances, it triggers action aimed at making amends or remedying harm done to ourselves or others.

According to Linehan (1993), developer of dialectic behavior therapy, emotional awareness is furthered when we observe and describe the phenomenological experience of our emotions, including the physical sensations they produce. For example, anxiety might be experienced as "butterflies in the stomach," anger may be felt as heat surging through the body, and sadness may be recognized as a painful lump or burning in the throat. Linehan (1993) also stressed the importance of identifying these feelings without "judging them or trying to inhibit them, block them, or distract from them" (p. 85). She pointed out that when we negatively evaluate our emotions, we add secondary feelings of guilt, anger, or anxiety to an already unpleasant situation. Conversely, when we relinquish this kind of judgment, we reduce the intensity of our suffering, while increasing our ability to tolerate distress.

When we are honest with ourselves about the expanse of our emotional repertoire, we are also on our way to emotional intelligence. Goleman (1998) contended that emotionally intelligent people have a deep understanding of their emotions and the effect they have on self, others, and job performance.

Your Emotional Repertoire

Review the list of emotions below and identify those that you have experienced over the last several weeks or months.

Affectionate	Disgusted	Joyful
Aggravated	Distressed	Lonely
Amazed	Eager	Mad
Amused	Embarrassed	Morbid
Anger	Enchanted	Nervous
Annoyed	Enraged	Outraged
Anxious	Euphoric	Overwhelmed
Apprehensive	Excited	Perturbed
Ashamed	Fearful	Petrified
Astonished	Fulfilled	Pleased
Bitter	Furious	Proud
Bored	Grateful	Rage
Calm	Grouchy	Remorse
Cheerful	Guilty	Resentful
Compassionate	Happy	Sad
Confident	Hopeful	Shame
Confused	Hopeless	Shock
Content	Horrified	Somber
Courageous	Hostile	Surprised
Curious	Humiliated	Thrilled
Cynical	Hurt	Tranquil
Dejected	Infuriated	Troubled
Delighted	Insecure	Tormented
Despair	Inspired	Unhappy
Determined	Intimidated	Upset
Disappointed	Irritated	Weary
Discouraged	Jealous	Worried

Consequently, they are often skilled and effective leaders in their organizations. These individuals are said to reveal candor and an ability to assess themselves realistically. They also display a willingness to "speak accurately and openly—although not necessarily effusively or confessionally—about their emotions and the impact they have on their work" (p.96). People with a high emotional IQ also appreciate the interplay between their thoughts and their emotional responses or reactions.

Reader Reflections

1) Which of the emotions listed in *Your Emotional Repertoire* have you had in recent days or weeks?
2) What physical sensations accompanied these emotions?
3) What events prompted them?
4) How did your behavior change as a result of your emotions?
5) What were the aftereffects of your emotional experiences?

Thinking about Your Thinking

In chapter 1, we noted that modern day humans are similar to other primates in their physiological response to acute stress. In this section, we focus on an aspect of being human that makes us distinct from other animals. Our ability to think about our thinking and problem solve accordingly is a capability that humans alone possess. Argyris and Schon (1974) referred to this mental process as *double loop learning*—a concept embedded in their theory of action perspective. They suggested that single-loop learning involves mastering the ability to act according to our assumptions about self, others, and situations. In contrast, double-loop learning entails an examination of the basic beliefs and assumptions that guide our behavior. This higher order type of learning allows one to avoid becoming a "prisoner of his programs" by considering alternative viewpoints, perspectives, and strategies for action (Argyris & Schon, 1974, p. 19).

To provide a forum for social workers to explore their thinking about the work they do, the clients they serve, and the systems in which they are employed, we performed workshops and focus groups across a wide range of organizational settings. We recruited social work employees, students, and volunteers from public and private nonprofit agencies that provide services to children in the child welfare system, youth or adults with mental health conditions, or victims of domestic violence. The purpose of the focus groups was to understand the stressful events that human service workers encounter on the job, their reactions to these events, and their preferred methods of coping. In addition, we collected written accounts from social work employees and students about their field experiences as they relate to workplace stress and various forms of client trauma. In the following pages, we share what we learned about the initial thoughts and reactions that workers reported having had in response to stressful encounters or conditions. This information is intended to serve as an aid for readers in identifying their own patterns of thinking in response to similar circumstances.

The workers we included in our project discussed a wide range of stressors that they confront on the job, including high caseload and administrative demands combined with on-going exposure to human suffering related to incidents of severe child abuse, domestic violence, suicide, homicide, and psychiatric or medical crises. Such incidents were often said to trigger feelings of profound sadness, helplessness, anger, and even disgust. These social workers also relayed occasions in which the social service and medical systems had failed to help their clients and placed roadblocks limiting access to needed care. Responses to these events included intense frustration and disappointment that "people who are supposed to help others don't."

Comments made by these social workers about such stressors reflect thinking patterns that fall into several broad categories. Some stress appraisals center on *harm* done by the troubling circumstance, consistent with the Lazarus and Folkman (1984) model discussed in chapter 1. For example, when faced with a victim of physical, sexual, or emotional abuse, most workers focus initially on the extent to which the person has been damaged, as seen in the following statements. "He was so innocent, now his trust has been demolished." "He probably has anger toward the universe." "I just imagined how much he suffered." "This poor person." "She is helpless." "How will she ever have a positive relationship again?" Other initial appraisals are devoted to *threat* posed by the stressor. For instance, when faced with a highly complex case-related issue, some workers worry about threats to their own feelings of competence or effectiveness, as seen in the following comments: "I am helpless in this situation," "If you don't know the answer you feel like an idiot because you think you should know the answer," and "Whatever I can do is not enough."

Initial stress appraisals also focus on three main areas of lack and limitation: *client-limitation, self-limitation,* and *system-limitation.* Client lack and limitation was the theme reflected in worker comments concerning the helplessness of victims and the depravity of abusers connected with their cases. In speaking about one mother on her caseload, a social worker described the woman's troubled past that included sexual abuse and involvement in the child welfare system. She reported that the woman was now drug addicted, had mental health problems, and had decided over and over to admit herself into a rehabilitation facility but could not actually do it. The worker said,

"It's really sad that the impact of her trauma wasn't dealt with when she was younger and now you see it repeat in her children." When writing about her interview with two preteen girls, a social work student noted her disgust with the girls' father who had sexually abused them and with their mother who had failed to protect them. She wrote: "I couldn't come to terms with why he would do such a terrible thing. I was relieved when he was left in jail awaiting trial. I wanted to find a way to not provide services to the mom. She had known all along that her daughters were in danger and she did nothing to help them. She didn't deserve to get services."

Self-limitation was a frequent topic in our focus groups, as seen in the following statements made about thoughts that arose during stressful encounters on the job: "I am not prepared for this" and "I might make a wrong decision." "I will be seen as weak for having these emotions." "I missed something and will be blamed." "What could I have done better last time I saw this client?" The tendency to beat oneself up for missed opportunities was clearly seen in one participant's comments regarding a case in which she, a child protective services worker, had placed children on her caseload in their grandmother's home, only to discover that one of them was later abused by the step-grandparent. "It was pretty traumatic—the child was thrown against the wall and there was a lot of bruising on his back . . . As I think back to the last few home visits that I made, I recall that they were at his day care center because it was more convenient . . . the grandparents worked late. I really thought the kids were ok in their home. Now, I look back and question myself. Maybe I should have done these visits in the grandparent's home. I ask myself what I could have done to prevent this. . . . yet, can I be perfect all the time?" In fact, some workers admitted that when expectations are great and more than they had bargained for when entering the field, they begin to question their ability to perform the job. The seeds of self-doubt can be seen in one participant's statement: "I sometimes wonder if I am really cut out for this profession"

Many workers also addressed system limitations that were apparent in situations in which their own or other agencies had exhausted their resources or neglected to help individuals in need. One discussed a phone call she received from a homeless victim of domestic violence who hung up once she heard that the shelter was full. "Someone calls for help and you do the best you can, but there really wasn't a lot to offer her. That never feels good." Another group participant spoke about the vulnerability of homeless women on her caseload. She stated, "There's no place for them to go except the library or the bookstore or someplace like that. They are not safe on the streets. It's really upsetting." Still another described a home visit he made to a filthy, emaciated older man who was drooling, having difficulty speaking and walking, and had not eaten in three days. The worker called for paramedics, as the man was clearly in need of medical care. He was shocked to find that when the paramedics arrived they were reluctant to deal with the older man, as they had a history with him in which he had been less than cooperative. At the social worker's insistence, the paramedics finally took the man into the ambulance and to the hospital. That incident left him with intense feelings of frustration that persisted for several days. Finally, another group member shared her outrage at the medical system when it failed to provide timely care for her mentally ill client. The woman she was helping had developed a cancerous tumor but had limited access to medical insurance. Consequently, she had to wait four and one-half months for a doctor's appointment from the time she was diagnosed. The worker stated, "My client felt sad and hopeless and I had a really hard time meeting with her every week and dealing with the injustice of it all."

Reader Reflections

Identify a recent work related situation that produced a strong stress reaction within you. Then answer the following:

1)   What thoughts did you have concerning client, self, or system limitation?
2)   Were you focused on harm done, threats posed, or challenges presented?

Making Meaning

In hearing the above accounts of highly stressful circumstances, we wondered if participating workers maintained these appraisals of harm, threat, and limitation over time. Through additional probing we learned that these initial appraisals did not tell the whole story about how meaning was made of such stress-inducing events. They do provide important insight into one component of the stress and coping process—the situational meaning that workers ascribe to specific work-related events. Park (2010) defined *situational meaning* as "meaning in the context of a particular environmental encounter" (p. 258). She contrasts it with *global meaning*, which is a

Catching Your Cognitions

We can think of our cognitions as assumptions acquired through perception, intuition, and reasoning. They include our appraisals of the significance of stressful events and circumstances. Review the following list of stress appraisals that other social workers report. Consider times when you have had the same or similar thoughts of lack and limitation as they relate to clients, yourself, and the systems that serve your clientele.

Limitation of Clients
- They are lost
- They are helpless
- They can't count on anyone
- They can't advocate for themselves
- They are damaged
- They are perverted
- They are undeserving of help

Limitation of Self
- I am helpless
- I am alone
- I am weak
- I am unprepared
- I am incompetent
- I am powerless
- I didn't do enough
- Whatever I do is not good enough

Limitation of Service Systems
- The system isn't working
- The system is not doing enough
- The system is hurting people
- The system doesn't back you up
- There is no accountability in the system
- People who are supposed to help others don't

more generalized level of meaning that encompasses a person's fundamental assumptions about the world, self, and self-in-the world. More specifically, global meaning comprises beliefs about order, predictability, benevolence, fairness, coherence in the world, and beliefs about one's own purpose and identity. This broader type of meaning is first developed early in life, yet

From the Field: When Everything You Did Is Still Not Enough

I'm going to tell a story, and it's an old story. There was a mom and dad on my caseload who were never married, but they had 8 children together. The last child was born drug addicted, put in foster care for two years, and later returned to his parents. Over the course of the next 5 to 10 years, he and his siblings were removed several times due to severe neglect and put into foster care. Finally, after a huge amount of work in supporting the youngest boy's adjustment to his foster home, he eventually became attached to his foster mother and was ultimately adopted by her. He turned 20 this last year, had severe kidney failure, and was on the list for kidney replacement. He then decided that since he was and adult, he didn't have to listen to his adoptive mother, so he moved out. He quit going to dialysis and reconnected with his birth mother who took possession of his SSI, his truck, and all his money. She established a place for them to live and then kicked him out. . . . He died. He had no care or assistance from his mother or anyone else when he passed. When I learned of his death, I thought about how the child welfare system had failed him. I wondered it there was something that we could have done to save him. Yet I also knew that we don't get to choose for the young adults in our system who have a will of their own. We were aware that his decision to go back to his bio mom was not a healthy one. However, he continued to say, "It's hard to stay away from Mom. It's just so hard."

—*Anonymous*

can be altered over time, and is said to "powerfully influence individuals' thoughts, actions, and emotional responses" (Park, 2010, p.258).

The meaning-making model advanced by Park and Folkman (1997) and later refined by Park (2010) explained the importance of both situational and global meaning in the stress-and-coping process. They contended that when we encounter a potentially stressful event, we immediately assess its situational meaning. If, however, the initial meaning made of the situation is incongruent with our global beliefs, distress is the likely result. This distress is said to trigger an additional step in the meaning-making process—one that is aimed at reducing the discrepancy between situational and global meaning. This step often involves reassessing, or reappraising, the event so that the world makes sense again. For example, if we have a fundamental belief in the basic goodness of human beings but are faced with a violent abuser whom we perceive as evil and corrupt, we will be motivated to rectify this

From the Field: When You Have No Clue What to Do

I had seen Maggie for over a year at a community-based counseling center. She was a 46-year old woman who had complex trauma due to both severe maltreatment that she had received as a child and physical abuse by her then husband. She was also suffering from grief related to the death of her child and sister. Years after our services ended she called me from a town that is about 200 miles away from my office. She was panicky, depressed, and said she needed help right away. I suggested that she call a mental health center in her area, but she refused. She then said she was "ok" and we agreed that I would call her the next day. Somewhere during this call, she gave me a description of her physical location. All that night I worried about her. I knew that she had a long history of suicidal thinking and some attempts. Yet, what could I do? The next morning as I listened to my voice mail messages, I heard two urgent calls from Maggie. I was able to reach her by phone and she still seemed very agitated. Yet, again, she insisted that she was "okay" and just needed some time to calm herself down. Then she hung up. I continued to feel very uneasy about all of her calls and her situation. I debated whether to contact law enforcement, as I wasn't sure if police contact would help the situation. After talking to my colleagues and supervisor, I decided to make the call. I contacted the police department in the town where she was located and requested a welfare check. I have not heard back from her since. I don't know if I did the right thing, but it was all I could think of to do. I can only hope that Maggie is really "okay."

—*Mary Ann*

discrepancy. Consequently, we may engage in a search for explanations for the abuser's noxious behavior (perhaps he himself was an abuse victim), or we might embrace a view of the person's abuse as more benign than that of other perpetrators. In chapter 4, we explore the reappraisals commonly used by social workers in coping with troubling workplace events. In this section, we encourage readers to explore their global beliefs and assumptions that play an important role in the meaning-making processes.

The concept of global meaning is consistent with constructivist self-development theory, as advanced by McCann and Pearlman (1990a). This theory maintains that we, as human beings, construct our own personal realities through the development of cognitive schemas that reflect our psychological needs for safety, dependency and trust, power, esteem, intimacy, independence, and frame of reference. These schemas consist of our beliefs and

Your Global Assumptions

The statements below are intended to help you assess your fundamental assumptions about yourself, others, and the world. Circle the answer that best represents your belief about each statement. Next, turn to Chapter Exercise #3 for guidance in further exploring the concept of global meaning.

- Life is predictable
  Never   Rarely   Sometimes   Usually   Always

- Life is fair
  Never   Rarely   Sometimes   Usually   Always

- People are basically good
  Never   Rarely   Sometimes   Usually   Always

- I am safe
  Never   Rarely   Sometimes   Usually   Always

- Most people are safe
  Never   Rarely   Sometimes   Usually   Always

- The world makes sense
  Never   Rarely   Sometimes   Usually   Always

- I am worthy of respect
  Never   Rarely   Sometimes   Usually   Always

- Others are worthy of respect
  Never   Rarely   Sometimes   Usually   Always

- I can trust others
  Never   Rarely   Sometimes   Usually   Always

- I have a purpose in life
  Never   Rarely   Sometimes   Usually   Always

- I have control over my life
  Never   Rarely   Sometimes   Usually   Always

- There is order in the world
  Never   Rarely   Sometimes   Usually   Always

expectations about self, others, and the world that help us make sense out of our experiences. For instance, if we enjoyed consistent care and attention from significant others early in life, we are likely to have developed core beliefs in the dependability and trustworthiness of others. Similarly, if we learned that independent action on our part was valued and reinforced, we likely developed a sense of self as autonomous. Finally, if we had limited direct experience with worldwide tragedy and suffering, we may have acquired an expectation that the world is basically safe and secure.

Both primary and secondary trauma can disrupt these schemas, leading us to feel less trusting of others, less safe in the world, less autonomous, more vulnerable, more focused on human perversity, more alienated, or even more disoriented (McCann & Pearlman, 1990b). There is ample evidence that direct exposure to traumatic events contributes to maladaptive core beliefs (van der Kolk, Roth, Pelcovitz, Sunday, & Spinazzola, 2005); there is less empirical support for the premise that secondary or indirect exposure to trauma leads to an altered worldview (Devilly, Wright, & Varker, 2009). In fact, in a recent study, Cox and Steiner (in press) found that some social workers, despite exposure to client suffering and trauma, demonstrate the ability to avoid schema disruption and preserve healthy global beliefs about self, others, and their profession. They do so through the use of tools and techniques discussed in the chapters to follow.

Conclusion

It is widely accepted that, as professional social workers, we must routinely engage in self-reflection if we are to avoid imposing our personal beliefs, values, and culturally acquired presumptions on the clients we serve. A less noted but equally important function of self-exploration is the recognition of key signs and symptoms of our own chronic stress related to social work. To further our self-awareness, it is essential that we attend to our emotions in response to difficult situations. Thinking about our thinking is also important, especially as it concerns our perceptions of harm, threat, and limitation. Such thoughts typically trigger upset, distress, and disillusionment. As we carry out this form of self-reflection, it is imperative that we use a gentle approach—one that avoids self-blame or self-loathing. Most would agree that success in self-care is established on the basis of a kind and compassionate view of self as a social worker.

Discussion Questions

1. What forces promote the use of harm and threat appraisals in social work? Give examples from your own field of practice.
2. Describe the difference between single-loop and double-loop learning. Why are both types of learning important in human services?
3. What is the difference between situational meaning and global meaning? Illustrate the difference with an example from your own experience.
4. How might constructivist self-development theory be used to guide a social worker's approach to self-care?
5. Which cognitive schemas have you seen disrupted in the clients you serve?

Chapter Exercises

1. Signs of Stress

Review the signs of stress in *What Are Your Signs of Stress?* Monitor your own stress responses over the next several weeks.

Do you tend toward physical, mental, emotional, or behavioral signs? Which ones?

2. Situational Meaning

Read the case example titled *From the Field: When Everything You Did Is Still Not Enough.* What reactions do have to reading this account? Emotions? Thoughts?

What might we learn from this young man's death?

If you were the primary worker on this case, how would you cope with this tragic situation?

3. Global Meaning

Complete the scale in *Your Global Assumptions.* Based on your ratings, what conclusions can you draw about your global assumptions? What life experiences have contributed to your fundamental beliefs about yourself, others, and the world?

Chapter 4
Self-Regulation

Whereas self-awareness establishes the foundation for self-care, self-regulation helps us achieve restoration following exposure to troubling work-related circumstances. It allows us to gain mastery over our thoughts and emotions so we can actualize our talents and maximize our success with clients. Strategies for fine-tuning this ability are important adjuncts to self-awareness, as self-insight alone often falls short of creating long-term personal change. It is widely accepted that if we are to overcome core beliefs that are known to impair functioning, we must learn how to redirect our thinking. We refer to this effort as *minding your mind*. Another commonly used approach to stabilizing emotions involves learning relaxation and mindfulness skills that are directed toward soothing the soul. A third, and vitally important aspect of self-regulation entails bringing in balance as it relates to the worker's approach to client care and empathy. Each of these key components of self-care is described in detail below with chapter exercises aimed at developing corresponding skills.

Minding Your Mind

Social workers experience a wide range of distressing events that could easily result in an orientation toward others that is negative, pessimistic, and judgmental. Such events also hold potential for triggering workers' doubts about their ability to make a difference in the lives of those they serve. Or, those events could prompt workers to view their clients as helpless, hopeless, or even undeserving of their time and attention. An antidote to this tendency can be found in the *cognitive reframe*, a powerful tool that reorients our view of people and problems so that they are seen in a more positive light. Watzlawick, Weakland, and Fitsch (1974) described reframing as a gentle art that involves placing a situation within another frame of reference that fits the facts "equally well or even better, and thereby changes its entire meaning" (p. 95). Folkman (1997) used the term *positive reappraisal* in referring to the process through which positive meaning is attached to disturbing circumstances. In her research, she found that this method of coping was associated with positive psychological states in caregiving partners of men with AIDS. A notable example of this coping tool was shown in the comments made by one participant in her study. A woman described her struggle with the repeated night sweats of her ailing husband, until she reframed it as an opportunity to demonstrate her love by providing needed care and nurturance. This shift in focus allowed her to experience warmth, as opposed to despair, in this difficult situation. Other research has identified similar benefits connected to the cognitive reappraisal. In a study of stress and coping processes evident in college students, Carver, Scheier, and Weintraub (1989) found that positive reinterpretation of stressful events is associated with self-esteem, hardiness, and reduced anxiety. More recently, Garnefski, Kraaij, and Spinhoven (2001) revealed the role of cognitive reappraisal in facilitating the regulation of moods and emotions in secondary school students. They found that greater use of this strategy for coping with life events was linked to fewer symptoms of depression and anxiety.

Learned optimism is recommended by Seligman (2006) as a means of enhancing overall quality of life as well as perseverance in the face of adversity. This involves adopting an "optimistic explanatory style" through which misfortune is interpreted as a temporary setback or challenge that can be overcome, as opposed to an indication of personal failure that is likely to persist or be permanent (p. 81). To break pessimistic habits and helpless attitudes, the individual is encouraged to dispute his or her negative beliefs and consider evidence that supports more constructive views. For example, a domestic worker who is fired by a disagreeable client might initially decide that this termination occurred because he or she is incapable and incompetent as an in-home assistant. To dispute this belief, the worker might consider alternative explanations for the client's anger. The worker might also recall times when he or she successfully managed domestic duties and satisfied clients. Through this process of disputation, the individual builds skills in optimistic thinking. Seligman (2006) cautioned, however, that there are limits to the benefits of a positive explanatory style. In fact, he argued that optimism should not be overblown or unrealistic—one must balance it with a need to see reality clearly and claim personal responsibility for mistakes or missteps.

From the Field: Finding Meaning in a Terrible Tragedy

BJ Miller was a sophomore in college when he climbed on an electrified shuttle train and received 11,000 volts of electricity (Yollin, 2011). As a result, he had his arm amputated below the elbow and lost both legs below the knee. Many people would have given up after this tragic experience. Not BJ—it made him more empathetic to the pain of others. Through it all he has remained passionate and engaged in his life and committed to giving back. He finished college and went on to medical school. He is the executive director of the Zen Hospice Project in San Francisco, where he helps patients manage pain and learn to accept their situations. When talking about what happened to him he stated, "I learned so much, particularly about perspective. It's not what you see, but how you see it" (Yollin, 2011, p. A14). He sees the silver lining in his accident in how it allows him to relate to and work with others who are suffering. "I'd always been aware that the way people treated me had nothing to do with my internal life. The world saw me as overprivileged. This changed all that. I didn't have to explain, 'Oh, I suffer too.' It was very handy" (Yollin, 2011, p. A14).

Recent work by Folkman (2008) provides additional guidance to those of us striving to adopt a more optimistic perspective. She offered a model that categorizes various *appraisal-based* or *meaning-focused coping* strategies that can be applied in stressful situations. On the basis of her own research and that of others, she identified five primary types of coping-based appraisals: benefit finding, benefit reminding, adaptive goal processes, reordering priorities, and infusing ordinary events with positive meaning. *Benefit finding* involves the discovery of positive effects that have resulted from distressing events. For instance, the death of a loved one may not only be found to produce sadness and despair but also a newfound appreciation for life and a sense of what is truly important. Other hardships may be recognized for their role in increasing strength, wisdom, and fortitude. *Benefit reminding* simply refers to the act of reminding oneself of the potential benefits of stressful situations as they are actually occurring. For example, a person who is dealing with a current family crisis might recall the way that previous challenges have increased closeness and connection within the family unit. *Adaptive goal processes* include weighing the odds of success or failure with particular goals and relinquishing those that are unrealistic or unattainable. Individuals might be adapting goals effectively when they give up trying to make abusive relationships work and focus instead on establishing new and better partnerships. Similarly, the *reordering of priorities* involves a shift in perspective about what really matters and where one should focus their effort and attention. For instance, a college student who is failing classes may decide that staying on course with their educational goals is more important than frequent partying with friends. Finally, *infusing ordinary events with positive meaning* entails attending to positive or pleasurable experiences on a day-to-day basis. Such ordinary experiences might include watching a sunset, connecting with a friend, or observing an act of kindness or consideration. These instances are said to provide a "psychological time-out" and a "momentary respite from on-going stress" (Folkman & Moskowitz, 2000, p. 116).

These cognitive coping strategies are often applicable to stressful circumstances encountered by workers in the human services field. In the focus groups described in chapter 3, we asked social workers to comment on the ways in which they make meaning of their experiences with client trauma or suffering. We also inquired as to ways in which benefit finding, benefit reminding, adaptive goal processes, reordering of priorities, and infusing ordinary events with meaning have been or might be helpful to them in managing work-related stress. Many reported the use of benefit finding when confronted with disturbing case-related events. For example, when made aware of the horrific

From the Field: Finding Benefits in a Bad Situation

About one year ago, a woman came into the shelter. She was really scared. She had been putting up with abuse from her husband for a long time. She had finally mustered up the courage to leave the home and strike out on her own, but only after he had seriously injured her. This woman's husband had taken a machete to her hand! I had a really hard time with this one. I didn't understand why she had chosen to stay with him, knowing how violent he was. The good news was that he was in jail. Over the next few months, I began to see that her injury was, in some ways, a blessing in disguise. It motivated her to get some help and end her abusive relationship once and for all. She went back to school and got a bachelor's degree. I saw her a while ago and found out that she is now working at the university and is in a much healthier relationship with her new boyfriend. She has never looked back. I was really happy for her. I think of this woman when I see others who have been harmed by partnership abuse. I remind myself that a serious injury is sometimes what people need to push them forward when they need to make a massive change in their life.

—*Anonymous*

abuse incurred by their clients, some shifted their thinking from the harm that had been done to the opportunities offered for change and improved safety and well-being for the trauma survivors. A clear example of benefit finding is seen in a worker's comments concerning an interview held with a depressed three-year-old child who had been sexually abused by a family member. The social worker said "It was very intense for me to know what happened to this innocent kid. Then I thought about how he is now going to get the help he needs." Another example is apparent in the statement made by a domestic violence worker about her client's serious injury at the hands of her partner. "It was a really scary situation but turned out to be a good thing because he went on to jail, and she was able to get a job." Also mentioned were benefits identified for the workers themselves as a result of stressful circumstances. When faced with a situation that they felt unprepared to handle, many focused on how they could learn and grow from the challenge that was presented. Such benefits are reflected in one participant's statement about an emotionally trying event: "I knew that I was growing from this experience as a professional and a person." Another worker found positive recognition in a very difficult interview with a client in pain. He stated, "What an honor it is that this person was willing to share with me something so personal and so troubling."

Benefit reminding is particularly useful in helping workers shift their thinking about self and system lack and limitation. It can be prompted by visual cues around the office, such as newspaper clippings or photographs that trigger memories of positive outcomes achieved. One worker was impressed with what she described as a "wall of victories" at her workplace, on which names were listed to memorialize successful cases. Another study participant recalled her appreciation for a picture drawn by a child on her caseload. The drawing, now posted in her office, depicts the child's family in "a good place" after stable housing had been located for them. Others mentioned the value placed on thank you notes and awards for a job well done. Such reminders help workers "hang on to their success stories," even during times of trial and tribulation.

Reader Reflections

1) What visual reminders of successful outcomes are present in your work environment?

2) What recommendations could you make for displaying additional benefit reminders in your office?

3) What support would you need to create this type of visual display?

Adaptive goal processes are seen when workers adjust their thinking about what constitutes a realistic service delivery goal. For instance, when providing brief collateral services to the parent of a child with emotional and behavioral problems, one worker accepted that it was highly unlikely that she would "cure" the parent of her self-disclosed borderline personality disorder; she had a greater likelihood of success in helping this mother acquire needed mood management and parenting skills. Similarly, many of the social workers in our study seem to redirect their focus away from things over which they have no control to things they can reasonably accomplish. They routinely remind themselves: "I am not wonder woman;" "I don't have a magic wand;" "I am planting seeds;" "It's my job to give my client's resources. I can't make them choose to use them!" Such resilient workers reorder their priorities, placing emphasis on doing their best, being fully present with their clients, and learning from their own mistakes.

The infusion of ordinary events with positive meaning on the part of social workers takes many different shapes and forms. For some, a typical drive home from work becomes a time of great release when a favorite song is played with the volume "cranked up." Others pay attention to the places and people for which they are thankful. Many use their free time in a ways that give them pleasure—caring for their animals, playing with their children, baking, or doing arts and crafts. Most find that laughter transforms everyday conversations into priceless points of contact and connection.

In addition to the five cognitive coping methods suggested by Folkman (2008), we found evidence of another strategy used by the social workers in our study. This strategy involves finding an acceptable reason for why a horrific event occurred, or a causal attribution (Park & Folkman, 1997). Attributions are explanations for behavior and events that aid us in making sense of our experiences. Workers go through a causal attribution process when they consider explanations for a person's aggressive or hurtful behavior. For instance, one participant in our focus groups discussed his initial disgust with a man who had sexually abused his grandson. The worker then considered the likely possibility that something "terrible happened to this grandpa to make him think that it was ok to do this to the boy." Another example is seen when social workers recognize that parents who are drug-addicted and neglectful of their children may have their own histories of abuse and trauma that they are replaying in their adult lives. A final illustration is seen when workers shift their perspective as it relates to disrespectful conduct or

Cognitive Reframes

We can think of our cognitive reframes as shifts in our perspective about stressful encounters or events. They often broaden our view to include new aspects of a situation, much as widening the frame on a photograph allows new visual elements to be seen. Review the following list of cognitive reappraisals that other social workers report. Consider times when you might adopt a similar type of reframe.

Stress Appraisal: Limitation of Client	Cognitive Reframe
"They are helpless"	"They are now getting the help they need"
"They are damaged"	"They can rebound from this hardship"
"They are evil/perverted"	"They have been victims themselves"

Stress Appraisal: Limitation of Self	Cognitive Reframe
"I am helpless"	"I am a helping tool"
"I am weak"	"I am human"
"I am incompetent"	"I am a work in progress"
"Whatever I do is not enough"	"I can make a start"

Stress Appraisal: Limitation of System	Cognitive Reframe
"The system isn't working"	"The system needs work"
"The system isn't doing enough"	"The system is overwhelmed"
"People who are supposed to help, don't"	"People do the best they can"

bullying on the part of colleagues. Instead of viewing the offensive coworker as inherently nasty and wicked, one might consider that he or she is insecure and feeling threatened by office politics. Such causal attributions do not excuse harmful acts, they merely allow us to understand where they may be coming from. This seems to ease our experience with troubling events and enhances our compassion for those who have behaved badly.

Reader Reflections

On the basis of your review of the cognitive reframes noted in *Cognitive Reframes,* answer the following:

1) When have you adopted stress appraisals that focus on the limitations of clients, yourself, or on the system as a whole?
2) What reframes might be useful to you in shifting your perspective?

Soothing the Soul

A common complaint of social workers is that they are "soul sick" as a result of job-related experiences that illuminate the devastating harm that can be done by one or more human beings toward others. In response to these encounters, workers sometimes become cynical and angry or melancholy and depressed as they begin to view the world as ugly, evil, and unsafe. One cure that has been prescribed for this condition is the practice of *mindfulness,* a state of being promoted by Eastern meditative traditions (Carmody, Baer, Lykins, & Olendzki, 2009). This practice is oriented toward increasing present moment awareness and producing a state of calm and contentment that counteracts reactivity, restlessness, and worry. Mindfulness training, now popular in the West as a clinical approach, contains two components: attention regulation and the adoption of an accepting attitude (Bishop et al., 2004). Attention regulation entails observing and recognizing bodily sensations, thoughts, and emotions in a detached manner. The practice of acceptance involves viewing current experience with curiosity and without judgment. Both skills are thought to enhance psychological well-being by blocking habitual reactions and promoting adaptive responses to stressful events. Research shows that mindfulness increases positive affect, decreases negative emotions (Schroevers & Brandsma, 2010), and supports self-esteem, life satisfaction, and optimism (Brown & Ryan, 2003). More specifically, it supports the use of positive reappraisals that contribute to adaptive coping (Garland, Gaylord, & Park, 2009).

Mindfulness is cultivated when certain attitudes are present, according to authors Stahl and Goldstein (2010). For example, a quality of nonstriving is said to be essential to mindfulness practice. This attitude entails giving up a desire to get anywhere other than you where you presently are and "letting be" (Stahl & Goldstein, 2010, p. 42). The importance of self-compassion is also recognized—the quality of caring for yourself and avoiding harsh self-criticism or self-blame. Finally, an orientation toward balance or equanimity is noted to be the key to greater wisdom and insight. This point is discussed by Linehan (1993) who suggested that we all have three primary states of mind: "reasonable mind," "emotion mind," and "wise mind." When we are centered in reasonable mind, we are thinking rationally and logically. Conversely, when we are centered in emotion mind, our thinking and behavior is controlled by our emotional state. The development of a wise mind involves integrating and balancing emotion mind and reasonable mind. This allows us to "add intuitive knowing to emotional experiencing and logical analysis" (Linehan, 1993, p. 63). Linehan (1993) encouraged the use of various mindfulness activities that help individuals attain this balance and participate in life with increased awareness.

Mindfulness-related activities are frequently focused on building present moment awareness through visual, auditory, and tactile means. Visual methods include taking the time to watch water flowing in a stream, snowflakes falling, or the leaves of a tree gently swaying in the breeze. Auditory methods might involve tuning into the sounds of a particular instrument playing in a favorite song, noticing the rhythms of birds singing outdoors, or listening to an audiotape of ocean waves breaking. Finally, tactile methods include focusing on your breathing; soaking in a warm bath; noticing the sensation of wind in your hair or sun on your face; slowly eating a meal while carefully attending to its smells, tastes, and textures. Individuals may be drawn to one primary type of mindfulness activity, whereas others benefit from a combination of these modes for enhancing sensory awareness.

In his book, *The Mindfulness Solution: Everyday Practices for Everyday Problems,* Siegel (2010) suggested that engaging in the above noted activities in a mindful way requires the ability to concentrate. This skill can be developed through formal practice in which we set aside time on a regular basis to "go to the mental gym" (Siegel, 2010, p. 43). We are encouraged to begin each practice session by focusing on an object of attention (visual, auditory, or tactile). Next, we notice when our mind has drifted from that object and we gently bring it back. Siegel (2010) argued that the key to successful mindfulness practice is finding the right level of effort. If we try too hard or are excessively rigid and strict with ourselves, our stress level can actually increase. Conversely, if we are too loose and undisciplined, we may have difficulty developing sustained attention. A balanced amount of effort can be found though trial and error. Chapter Exercise 2 is focused on helping the reader initiate mindfulness practice.

Mindfulness Activities

Visual Practices
- Notice the colors in your immediate surroundings
- Watch the movements of birds, animals, reptiles, insects
- Observe the sights as you drive your car
- Watch the "snow" falling in a snow globe or "lava" in a lava lamp
- Notice the clothing, movement, and facial expressions of the people you see
- Attend to the weather outdoors (sun shining, rain/snow falling, wind blowing)

Auditory Practices
- Listen closely to the sound of birds chirping, dogs barking, cats meowing
- Attend to one instrument playing in a song or musical piece
- Notice the sounds made by children playing
- Listen with acceptance to unpleasant sounds (traffic, horns, sirens)
- Sit in silence

Tactile Practices
- Engage in slow, conscious breathing
- Stretch your body and attend to your movements
- Pay attention to sensations when walking (feet touching ground, legs in space)
- Notice the texture of your clothes, sheets, blankets
- Take in the smells of lotions, soaps, oils
- Notice the sensation of water covering your body when you shower or bathe
- Eat slowly, taking the time to smell, taste, and appreciate the texture of food

Reader Reflections

After reviewing *Mindfulness Activities,* answer the following:

1) Which practices are you drawn to for increasing sensory awareness?
2) What are the best times of day for you to practice mindfulness?
3) How might you build such activities into your daily routine?
4) What benefits might you achieve by monitoring your experience with mindfulness practice? (see Chapter Exercise 2 for a suggested format)

Another strategy recommended for self-soothing involves increasing ones connectivity with others. Creating meaningful connections leaves you and others feeling noticed, respected, and highly regarded. This effort can be as simple as sharing a smile and kind word with a client who is waiting in the reception area of the office. In this way we are infusing an ordinary event with meaning. Other options include "nurturing colleagueship" in the workplace by sharing experiences with coworkers and hearing, while validating, theirs (Saakvitne & Pearlman, 1996, p. 79). In fact, the professional peer group is recognized as an important resource for practitioners, providing access to tangible aid, acceptance, and an objective yet informed perspective concerning the realities of the social worker's job (Catherall, 1999). In support of this view, a study of 188 trauma therapists revealed that 85% believe that discussing cases with colleagues is helpful to them in coping with the stresses associated with their work (Pearlman, 1999). In their book devoted to trauma stewardship, van Dernoot Lipsky and Burk (2009) stressed the importance of creating a "microculture" or chosen group of people who provide us with nurturing and encouragement. They stated that members of the group should be those that we can "debrief with, laugh with, brainstorm with, consult with, cry with, and become better people with" (van Dernoot Lipsky & Burk, 2009, p. 185).

For some workers, connectivity also refers to their relationship with an ultimate, omnipresent power or God. Maintaining a spiritual life helps them to maintain a positive worldview and cope with the demands of their work. Involvement in faith-based groups, prayer, meditation, or yoga can prove beneficial by renewing a sense of purpose, compassion, forgiveness, and hope. Spending time in nature is also recognized for its ability to help us tune into "the harmonious interaction of all the elements and forces of life" and achieve a "sense of unity with all" (Chopra, 1994, p. 18). Such connections provide a powerful means of soothing the soul.

Bringing in Balance

A variety of general approaches have been previously offered for bringing balance to the life of social workers. Recommendations include creating balance between work, play, and rest activities so as to enhance a sense of personal integration (Saakvitne & Pearlman, 1996). Workers are also encouraged to balance their caseload to include both complex cases with trauma survivors and less intense ones with nonsurvivors, balance their workday between direct service activities and administrative functions, and take time each day for relaxation (Pearlman, 1999). These suggestions are not without merit; however, we argue that another type of balance is equally important to self-regulation: balanced use of empathy.

It is generally accepted that one of the greatest tools that social workers bring to their craft is the capacity to respond to others with empathy. Novice practitioners are taught the importance of being "empathetically attuned" to their client's inner feelings and emotions (Hepworth, Rooney, Dewberry Rooney, Strom-Gottfried, & Larsen, 2010, p. 88). Yet, without a clear understanding of the dynamics of empathy, these practitioners may succumb to the unseen dangers that lurk within an unbridled or uncontrolled use of this device. Several approaches have been taken to illuminate the meaning of *empathy*. Merriam-Webster (2012) defines it as "the action of understanding, being aware of, being sensitive to and vicariously experiencing the feelings, thoughts, and experience of another of either the past or present, without having the feelings, thoughts, and experience fully communicated in an objectively explicit manner." Raines (1990) offered a historical perspective, noting that the word *empathy* originates from the German term *einfuhling*, defined as "to feel into" the experience of another person. In applying this concept to clinical practice, he suggested that when workers let their defenses down, they are able to "feel the client's feeling reverberate within (their) own being," thus enabling them to recognize that they share the same basic fears and insecurities (Raines, 1990, p. 70). As a result, social workers are prepared to offer genuine acceptance to the individual with whom they are establishing a helping relationship. Buie (1981) concurred that human service workers commonly reflect on their own personal memories to get a handle on what the client is experiencing. Problems arise, however, when workers over-identify with their clients and take on their anger, anxiety, or despair. Moreover, a loss of empathetic control occurs when what appears to be empathy is actually an overinvolved response to the client that is rooted in the personality or unmet emotional needs of the human services practitioner (Greenson, 1960).

Finding balance between empathy for others and the need to stand apart from their pain is the key to self-care in social work. Appreciation for this challenge can be found in the ancient myth of Shiva, the Hindu God of Dance and Death. Legend holds that Shiva was a strict yogi who lived in the mountains of India. He had renounced worldly pleasures until lured into marriage by Parvati, a beautiful young maiden. The relationship that evolved between Shiva and his wife is thought to represent the tension between the ascetic or spiritual ideal and domestic life that includes marriage, sex, and children.

Lord Shiva learned to do the dance between both worlds—he became both a part of and apart from the domestic world with his family. In a similar way, social workers need to join with their clients and establish an empathetic bond, while also standing apart from the trauma and suffering that is part of the clients' life experience. This is a very delicate dance but one that can be learned and practiced. Chapter Exercise 3 is intended to guide readers in balanced used of empathy.

Reader Reflections

1) When have you overidentified with or become overinvolved with a client?
2) What did you notice about how this affected your effectiveness?
3) What helps you to maintain balance in your use of empathy?

Often, however, when social workers are emotionally entangled with their clients, untamed countertransference is at work. The concept of *counter-transference* originated in psychoanalytic practice but has received ample attention across a variety of approaches to clinical social work. It refers to the unconscious needs, feelings, and wishes that the practitioner projects onto the client (Brenner, 1985). In extreme cases, such repressed emotions can move "beyond empathy through identification toward distortion" as the worker becomes lost in the therapeutic relationship (Southern, 2007, p. 280). Hayes (1995) offered a framework for conceptualizing counter-transference that highlights the importance of its triggers, manifestations, effects, and management. This model suggests that the origins of the phe-nomenon are found in the clinician's unresolved psychological conflicts or issues. These issues are triggered by service-related events and are manifested in the worker's thoughts, feelings, and behaviors that, in turn, have effects on the therapeutic process. The management of countertransference requires insight, emotion-regulation skills, and other forms of self-care that are neces-sary to keep it in check.

According to Wilson, Lindy, and Raphael (1994), there are two main types of countertransference reactions. Type I is said to include avoidance, detach-ment, and withdrawal from the client to minimize emotional pain triggered by the therapeutic process. Type II includes overidentification and overin-volvement, along with a tendency to take excessive responsibility for the client's healing and recovery. Both types of reactions are said to intensify when the helping relationship is characterized by empathetic strain. Access to quality supervision is critical in furthering the effective management of countertransference. An attuned supervisor is adept at exploring both Type I and Type II reactions and uses the supervisory process to help the social worker " hold the empathic bond and accept the limits of professional practice" (Southern, 2007, p. 290). Thus, he or she guides supervisees in bringing balance to their working relationships with clients. When such balance is out of reach, referrals for personal counseling to address the underlying conflicts and psychological issues of the practitioner may be needed.

It is important to recognize, however, that countertransference is not inherently bad. In fact, it is a normal and natural occurrence that can yield great benefits when accepted and understood. Most self-aware social workers will readily admit to times in which a client managed to push their buttons and

From the Field: Encountering Countertransference

I was a clinical social worker employed at a juvenile justice facility. I had been doing individual and group counseling with Megan (age 14) for several months and had become aware of this girl's depression, low self-esteem, and anger toward her mother. So I held a family session with Megan and her mother (Julia) to explore the roots of their conflicted relationship. From the start of the meeting, I saw the emotional distance between the two. There was little eye contact between them and Julia did most of the talking while Megan appeared to "check out." What was most disturbing was that Julia was highly critical of her daughter, even belittling at times, and had nothing complimentary to say about her. This mother focused the conversation on her own life-long emotional challenges and appeared oblivious to her daughter's need for her acceptance and approval. Following the session, I found myself feeling agitated and angry. I was so irritated with Julia that I didn't want to set up another meeting with her. Later that week I talked to my supervisor about this case and shared my feelings toward Julia. He asked me what about this mother was triggering my intense emotions. After some thought, I put the pieces together. I realized that the dynamics between Megan and Julia were strikingly similar to those I shared with my own mother. I reflected further and saw that I was still carrying some resentment about my own mother's perpetual, albeit well-intended, criticism of me. Then I got really honest with myself and recognized that I myself had a somewhat critical nature, which is something I was trying hard to overcome. This understanding helped me relate more compassionately with Julia in later sessions that I had with her.

—Frances

trigger their own unresolved issues. When this occurs, a wonderful opportunity is presented to practitioners to examine their personal struggles and identify the source of their reactions. In doing so, they may discover that what they find distasteful in others is what they also find distasteful in themselves. Ideally, this insight will guide helpers in developing a greater level of compassion for themselves as well as the individuals whom they serve.

Conclusion

The regulation of one's own thoughts and emotions is a commonly overlooked yet essential component of self-care. There are a variety of strategies that can be used to manage thinking and help the social worker find positive meaning in distressing work-related events. Self-soothing also makes important contributions to the management of emotions, and participation in mindfulness activities can help practitioners relieve stress and enhance relaxation. Finding balance in life is also essential to the self-care process. Balance, as it relates to the professional helper's emotional involvement with clients, is particularly important. It is safe to assume that social workers are much better prepared to help others achieve balance and stability if they have reached a state of balance in their own lives.

Questions for Discussion

1. What do you see as the benefits and challenges associated with learned optimism? How might you apply this concept to your work?
2. How do workers in your field of practice adapt service delivery goals so that they are realistic and achievable?
3. How might connectivity between colleagues be furthered in your agency? What barriers might be encountered in working toward this goal?
4. How do practitioners balance empathy for others with the need to stand apart from their pain? What challenges have you faced in doing so?
5. Are you more inclined toward Type I or Type II countertransference? Illustrate your answer with an example.

Chapter Exercises

1. Stress Appraisals

Review the stress appraisals noted in *Cognitve Reframes*. List those that you have made (regarding clients, yourself, or system limitations), along with accompanying cognitive reframes.

2. Mindfulness

Read the mindfulness activities listed in *Mindfulness Activities*. Select some visual, auditory, and tactile methods for enhancing your sensory awareness. Take time each day over the next two weeks to carry out one of these activities (5 to 10 minutes each) with moment-to-moment awareness. Keep a record of your affect/mood during and after these practices. Which method was most helpful in producing a state of calm and contentment?

3. Balanced Use of Empathy

List several of the most distressing experiences you have had when exposed to client trauma or suffering. Now, close your eyes and visual one of these client's speaking about the trauma they have endured. Pay particular attention to their body language, tone of voice, facial expressions and posture. Now imagine yourself saying to this person "I care about you and your suffering but need to stand apart from your pain if I am to be helpful to you." Visualize yourself drawing a circle around where you and your client are standing. Then see yourself stepping outside the circle. Notice that your client is pleased that you have taken this important step. Recognize the emotions and beliefs you let go of, as a result of this movement. Now repeat this visualization with every traumatized client you identified.

Chapter 5
Self-Efficacy

The field of social work is fraught with menacing circumstances that can whittle away at our feelings of competence, if we let them. We are often faced with unreasonable demands and uncontrollable conditions. Many times we are expected to achieve miracles, when it is clear that none are to be had. Often we are provided with inadequate resources to achieve the results we desire. Despite these challenges, it is vitally important that we acquire and maintain a sense of self-efficacy. It is what will enable us to persist in the face of what may appear to be insurmountable work-related obstacles. In this chapter, we discuss the concept of self-efficacy and its benefits. We also present threats to perceived efficacy identified in the literature and by participants in the focus groups we conducted, as described in chapter 3. Finally, we discuss ways to combat these threats and achieve increasing levels of self-confidence as social workers.

What Is Self-Efficacy?

According to Bandura (1997), *self-efficacy* refers to the judgments we make of our personal capability to carry out particular activities and produce positive results. It is a key component of our power to make things happen in the various domains of our lives. However, as Bandura (1997) pointed out, self-efficacy concerns not just the number of skills we possess, but rather what we believe we can do with the skills we have to serve our intended purposes. This distinction becomes clear when we consider that two people with the same skills may perform at markedly different levels in a particular situation. One with strong perceived effectiveness is likely to outperform one who harbors doubt about his or her capabilities. Bandura (1997) also made clear that self-efficacy is distinct from *self-esteem,* a concept that relates to our more generalized feelings of self-worth. In fact, he stated, "there is no fixed relationship between beliefs about one's capabilities and whether one likes or dislikes oneself" (p. 11). He maintained that we need much more than high self-esteem to perform well in a particular endeavor. A belief in our own effectiveness is required if we are to initiate and sustain attempts at coping with challenging or threatening situations. In fact, a strong sense of efficacy is needed "to remain task-oriented in the face of pressing situational demands, failures, and setbacks that have significant personal and social repercussions" (Bandura, 1995, p. 6).

Efficacy beliefs have been shown to influence our thoughts, feelings, and levels of motivation, along with our actions. On a cognitive level, they affect a variety of thinking patterns. For example, the stronger one's perceived efficacy, the more likely he or she is to assume a future time perspective, set challenging goals, and firmly commit himself or herself to them (Bandura, 1997). Efficacy beliefs also play an important role in the regulation of our emotions. When perceived efficacy is high, individuals believe that they can exercise some control over threatening events. Thus, they are less likely than those with low self-efficacy to display a high degree of fear and anxiety. Strong efficacy beliefs also serve to enhance motivation by supporting the view that increased effort is likely to pay off and help us attain desired results. Through these mediating processes, self-efficacy is believed to affect our performance in stressful circumstances.

Why Does Self-Efficacy Matter?

It seems reasonable to assume that the self-efficacy of human service workers contributes to their productivity and functioning and that of their organizations. Research conducted in recent years has supported this conjecture. One study examined the role of self-efficacy in buffering the effects of critical incidents on emergency workers. Results showed that workers with high self-efficacy were less affected by high-stress conditions and exhibited reduced levels of burnout and compassion fatigue (Prati, Pietrantoni, & Cicognani, 2010). In an exploratory study of social workers serving HIV-affected families, Letteney (2010) found that perceived self-efficacy was significantly related to comfort level in providing future care and custody services. Other studies have linked self-efficacy to reduced turnover in social workers. For example, Pincus (1997) found lower levels of attrition in school social workers that held the belief that they made a positive difference in their students and school system. Similarly, Caselman and Brandt (2007) found that the intent to stay employed on the part of school social workers was associated with high self-efficacy. In a large-scale study of child welfare workers (N = 941), Ellett (2009) examined several factors related to the intent to remain employed. Findings revealed that self-efficacy was positively associated with a high level of human caring; both self-efficacy and human caring were linked to the intent to remain employed in child welfare.

Threats to Self-Efficacy in Social Work

Some social workers may be surprised to learn that many of the most powerful threats to our self-efficacy come from within. Yes, organizational pressures and practices can affect our feelings of competence, and in later chapters we explore these challenges. In this chapter, we focus on the misguided beliefs and faulty assumptions that contribute to our perceptions of inadequacy. Ellis (1984) discussed several of these common cognitive errors in his book *How to Deal With Your Most Difficult Client—You*. Here he lists five *musturbations*, or irrational things therapists and other professional helpers tell themselves about what they must do or what should occur during their clinical practice. First, is the belief that one must be successful with their clients almost all of the time. This assumption is bound to result in disappointment, as success in social work is not universal or all-inclusive. It is unrealistic for any of us to assume that we will achieve positive outcomes with all the clients we serve. Consider the fact that we may spend an hour a week for several months with clients who have spent many years in unhealthy environments. Clearly, it is unreasonable to expect that we will make substantial changes in all of these clients' lives, given the limited amount of time they are with us.

Second on Ellis's (1984) list of musturbations is the notion that we must be one of the world's most outstanding practitioners. By holding this belief, we set ourselves up for frustration, as we can all find someone who is better trained or equipped than ourselves to deal with highly complex cases. Third on the list is the assumption that we must be liked and respected by all our clients. For those of us working with clients who are court mandated to receive services, this objective is clearly unattainable. Such clients may be hostile and resentful from the start of our very first contact. Even with voluntary clients, we often must address painful topics that can trigger their feelings of anger and upset. Thus, the interactions we have with the individuals we serve are not likely to be experienced as "warm and fuzzy" most of the time.

A fourth misguided assumption is the belief that because we are hard-working, our clients should be equally persevering. Of course we would prefer that all of our clients dedicate themselves wholeheartedly to the process of treatment or recovery. However, the reality is that they come to us at varying levels of readiness for change. Whereas some are fully prepared to commit to a treatment plan, many others have barely begun to recognize the need to address a problem or alter their behavior. Consequently, there may be a "readiness gap between them and us" as it concerns the change process (Skovholt & Trotter-Mathison, 2011, p. 108). It is very important that this gap be recognized and understood. If strategies for enhancing client motivation are unsuccessful, we need to accept that every individual has a right to choose how they want to live their own life. In fact, the NASW (2008) *Code of Ethics* (standard 1.02) asserts that we must respect our clients' right to self-determination—this includes the right to decide how much to invest in the service delivery process. Another version of this musturbation is the belief that because we are dedicated and committed to our clients, other professionals should be equally so. Workers who maintain this perspective often find themselves fixated on the lack of investment or other failings of colleagues or other human services providers with whom they come in contact. They may even ruminate about being associated with a system that is flawed and ineffective. Consequently, their mental and emotional resources are habitually expended. A final musturbation is the belief that we must be able to enjoy ourselves during our practice. This somewhat entitled assumption may result in our using only the strategies and techniques we enjoy, thereby limiting our effectiveness in situations that call for a different approach. Ellis (1984) recommended that we counter this belief by accepting that work-related conditions "don't *have to be* always easy, comfortable, and enjoyable" (p. 4).

Additional misguided beliefs have been observed in professional helpers by Norcross and Guy (2007). For instance, *selective abstraction* is a pattern of faulty thinking that is said to plague even the most experienced clinicians. This orientation assumes that the most important events are our failures and that we should evaluate ourselves by our mistakes (Beck et al., 1979). Practitioners who embrace this view are often preoccupied with what they have done that did not work versus what they have accomplished. They typically strive for perfection and have difficulty accepting their own inevitable limitations. As a result of their unrealistic expectations of self, these workers are likely to experience a high degree of mental stress and suffering. *Assuming causality* is another commonly held cognitive distortion in which

Replacing Thoughts that Threaten Self-Efficacy

Review the faulty assumptions listed in the column to the left and consider times when you have had these or similar thoughts. Then consider the benefits of adopting the replacement thoughts as they relate to your work.

Faulty Beliefs by Practitioners	Replacement Thoughts
• I must be great at everything that I do	• I can be "good enough" at some of the things that I do
• If my client fails, it must mean that I have failed	• There are many factors that influence my client's success or failure
• My case is all screwed up	• My case has some difficult challenges
• If my coworker yells at me, I must be to blame	• My coworker's anger many not be about me
• The worst is bound to happen	• What are the real probabilities that the worst will occur?
• I must be the best at the things I do	• I want to do the best that I can
• I can't screw up	• I can learn from my mistakes

one incorrectly assigns "the blame or responsibility for adverse events to themselves" (Norcross & Guy, 2007, p. 123). Social workers who fall prey to this perception may personalize the negative emotions of their clients or colleagues. In addition, they may readily assume that they are at fault when a case goes sideways. Perpetual anguish is the likely result of their tendency to take the blame for situations over which they have little or no control. Next, *catastrophizing* is said to be at work when we expect the very worst outcomes from challenging or stressful events. This inclination to predict doom makes it difficult for us to maintain a sense of hope that conditions can change or improve. It is a form of faulty thinking that can contribute to high anxiety and a self-fulfilling prophecy of failure. Finally, *dichotomous thinking,* or a black-or-white perspective, can be a roadblock for personal efficacy. This type of extreme thinking leads us to view situations as either all good or all bad. It limits our ability to see the "gray areas" and to recognize steps toward success and partial gains in our competence and skill.

Reader Reflections

After reviewing the thoughts that threaten self-efficacy listed in *Replacing Thoughts that Threaten Self-Efficacy,* answer the following:

1) Which of these faulty assumptions have you held?
2) Which of these faulty beliefs have you noticed in colleagues?
3) What replacement thoughts might be helpful, as they relate to your work?

In the focus groups held with social work practitioners, as described in chapter 3, we found evidence of another cognitive pattern that may threaten self-efficacy—the *rescue fantasy*. This term was first applied to the mental health practitioner by Greenacre (1971) in her work on countertransference. She believed that the latent rescue fantasy embodies the therapist's need to be "the sympathetic parent through whom the patient will find a complete cure, approximating even a rebirth" (Greenacre, 1971, p. 760). Social work practice with children and adolescents may be particularly fertile ground for the development of such fantasies. Here, the helping professional forms a therapeutic relationship with youth who are suffering, sometimes because of the mistreatment or neglect of their parents or other caregivers. In some cases, child practitioners become overidentified with a youth and construct unrealistic daydreams in which they are the child's savior and the caregiver is the villain to be conquered or overcome (Malawista, 2004). This tendency was apparent in focus group participants who reported a wish to take a child home with them to provide him or her with a better life. Although this type of rescue fantasy is completely understandable, it is not without cost. One consequence is that it establishes an unconscious competition between the service provider and the child's parent. Another is that the worker's own perceived efficacy is potentially jeopardized, as whatever is accomplished through professional service delivery is no match for the fantasized version of helping.

Sustaining Self-Efficacy

As we approach the development of self-efficacy, it is important to recognize that it is not an end state but, rather, an evolving evaluation of self as competent in social work. This evolutionary nature of self-efficacy becomes clear when we consider that fledgling social workers might be self-satisfied with their acquisition of basic interviewing skills and knowledge of agency

From the Field: My Fantasy of Rescue

My client was a little 7-year-old girl named Krystal who I had been seeing weekly for home-based therapy. She had been in and out of foster care and was now back in her mother's custody. As a result of her traumatic background, Krystal had lots of attachment issues. It was hard for her to trust anyone and she had tantrums when scolded by her mother or her stepfather. One day when I arrived at the apartment, Krystal was crying in the kitchen and staring at the wall. When she saw me, she cried, "Please take me outta here! I don't want to be here. I am scared and they are not talking to me". Then Krystal's mother told me that they were ignoring her. In fact, the whole family had made a plan to ignore her, as they didn't want her to make a child abuse report as she had done in the past. Right in front of the little girl, the parents said that they wanted her removed from the home because they didn't feel safe. "She needs to know the truth about what we are doing, that we want her to be moved. She's going to be a psychopath when she gets older, you know!" Wow, I had a really hard time witnessing this situation and holding myself together. I wanted to jump in and take Krystal home with me, but I knew I couldn't. All I could do was call CPS, which I did. I waited for the police to come and take her to a voluntary placement. It was very sad. But I focused on the fact that I had done the best I could, given the circumstances.

—*Anonymous*

policies and procedures. Over time, these same workers might focus their self-appraisals on their capacity to use more advanced practice skills and to produce positive outcomes in highly complex cases. Even later on in their careers, these workers might evaluate their capability on the basis of skill in performing supervision with other social workers. Yet, no matter where a social worker is in his or her professional development, self-efficacy needs to be nurtured and supported. In the following paragraphs, we suggest several strategies for doing so. To provide a foundation for this discussion, we present a brief overview of the literature concerning the primary sources of perceived efficacy.

Much has been written about how we acquire self-efficacy. Bandura (1997) identified several primary sources: enactive mastery, vicarious experiences, verbal persuasion, and physiological and affective states. *Enactive mastery* is considered the most influential source of perceived efficacy. It involves repeated performance-based indicators of competence that are evident despite hardship. This form of mastery may occur for the social worker who carries a challenging caseload yet receives on-going data confirming that his or her clients have attained positive outcomes or have expressed a high level of satisfaction with services. *Vicarious experiences* increase self-efficacy when we observe others in action and decide that we too can master similar activities. Such experiences also contribute to efficacy beliefs when we positively appraise our own ability in comparison with others. *Verbal persuasion* may enhance efficacy beliefs when significant others express confidence in our capability to master certain activities or tasks. Positive feedback from a supervisor or colleague can increase a social worker's feelings of competence, particularly when it is based on concrete evidence or in-person observation of performance. Finally, *physiological and affective states* provide us with another basis for evaluating our own capability. When we become tense or agitated in a stressful situation, we are less likely to expect success. We know from experience that such stress reactions impair our performance. Fatigue, aches and pains, and negative emotions may trigger beliefs regarding our vulnerability in response to challenging circumstances. Conversely, feelings of relative calm combined with physical stamina can contribute to confidence in our ability to overcome adversity.

Strategies that support and sustain self-efficacy in social work are helpful, in part, because they provide expanded opportunities for enactive mastery, vicarious experiences, verbal persuasion, and the management of physiological and affective states. In the pages to follow, several methods are proposed and referred to as "celebrating small steps," "prioritizing process," and "cultivating competence." All three are intended to assist workers in overcoming the commonly experienced barriers to perceived effectiveness that we discussed in the previous section. Each encourages workers to consider what may be new and different ways of thinking about and approaching their practice.

One way to battle threats to self-efficacy is to adopt realistic goals and objectives for our work with clients and client systems. This is an important element in meaning-focused coping, as we noted in chapter 4. Yet it sometimes runs counter to our profession's longstanding tendency to strive for huge transformation in the communities and populations we serve. In 1974, Briar referred to the "formula for frustration" that is advanced in social work when we proclaim unattainable goals (for example, the goal to end poverty that was prominent in the 1960s) (p. 518). He argued that it is not enough to know where we want to go—we must also know how to take steps toward that destination. Although ultimate goals point us in the right direction, it is vital that we identify feasible and proximate objectives. In so doing, we clarify a path to success and set the stage for our celebration of small steps toward long-term goals. Briar's (1974) advice is still relevant in the 21st century.

Hepworth and colleagues (2010) stress the importance of partializing goals in social work and dissecting them into "manageable portions" (p. 315). Clearly, when we break larger goals down into smaller pieces, we enable an on-going focus on signs of success and indicators of competence that are required for enactive mastery, a central source of self-efficacy. A focus group participant provided an excellent example of the use of this skill. She discussed having taken on a newly created social work position that was designed to "bridge the gap" between various human services agencies. The expectations for her role seemed overwhelming, particularly given that interagency tension and conflict had been going on long before she took the job. The worker admitted to feelings of frustration and irritability at times but also relayed a sense of optimism. She was able to move forward by avoiding a tendency to blame herself and others for the troubles encountered. She focused on clear-cut tasks and objectives that could be accomplished, such as having cooperative conversations with interagency partners, conducting successful multidisciplinary meetings, and linking clients with cross-agency resources. Moreover, this social worker recognized and relished each of these little victories when they occurred. She clearly knew how to celebrate small steps toward her long-term goals.

Reader Reflections

1) Consider a big goal that you have for your work and how you might break it down into smaller victories.
2) How might you celebrate these steps toward success?
3) How can you help your colleagues to celebrate small steps toward long-term goals?

The *prioritizing process,* a similar strategy, involves recognizing the value in a high-quality service that we have performed, even when positive outcomes are beyond reach or unlikely to occur in the near future. In keeping with this theme, social workers frequently refer to their role in "planting seeds." This is an apt metaphor in that we are often called on to share concepts and ideas with individuals, groups, communities, or colleagues that are not yet ready to embrace them. We are similar to the gardener who works hard to test, till, and fertilize the soil for a tiny vegetable plant, not knowing for sure if these efforts will bear fruit. He cannot control many of the other variables that determine the health and well-being of the vegetable—the temperature, precipitation, or sunlight. Like the social worker, he can merely do his best to be productive with the skill and resources he has at his disposal.

For human service practitioners, prioritizing process can be especially helpful when cases are complex and clients are fearful of change. For instance, when serving families in which there have been multigenerational challenges with mental illness, substance dependence, domestic violence, or child abuse and neglect, progress can seem painstakingly slow. The notion of giving up destructive yet familiar ways might be experienced as threatening to such clients, even when they are faced with pressures from law enforcement or child protection agencies. Sometimes, the best we can do is validate the family members' pain, help them recognize their ambivalence about making change, and offer tangible aid (for example, access to transportation, medical care, or a domestic violence shelter) to support them in their recovery. When we are able do so with patience and skill, we can take pride in our process, even though the client may not be ready for the level of change we would ultimately like to see.

Finally, efforts toward cultivating competence are essential to the promotion of self-efficacy. Such endeavors almost always entail risk taking: acknowledging the need for additional knowledge and skill, hearing feedback about performance, and accepting suggestions for improved practice. The reality of risk is particularly true of efforts made to acquire skill in the use of an evidence-based model of practice. Training in these models typically includes not only the review of a treatment manual and attendance at didactic presentations, but also group supervision and individual coaching. Supervisory sessions often include role-play demonstrations, observation of trainee interviews, or the review of audio or videotaped client sessions by consulting experts. When social workers avail themselves of this type of live supervision and skill-based coaching, they are likely to acquire a high level of skill. Moreover, their efficacy beliefs are enhanced through vicarious experience as well as the verbal persuasion they receive concerning their ability to implement a particular approach to practice. In fact, research has shown that direct supervision of casework (Sholomskas et al., 2005) and expert feedback (Henggeler, Melton, Brondino, Scherer, & Hanley, 1997; Henggeler, Schoenwald, Letourneau, & Edwards; 2002) are important adjuncts to didactic seminars in supporting the successful adoption of empirically supported models of practice.

From the Field: Planting Seeds with Sammy

I had been working with Sammy for 6 months. He was a resident in a treatment facility for youth offenders. I was a clinical social worker who provided him with individual, group, and family therapy. He was an angry teen who had been seriously abused by his father as a young boy. As a result, he had symptoms of posttraumatic stress, including nightmares and flashbacks. Sammy also struggled with intense guilt because, just prior to his commitment to the facility, he had retaliated toward his father in a big way. He pulled a shotgun on him and fired, leaving his dad as a wheelchair-bound paraplegic. Therapy with Sammy was intense and culminated in a meeting between his father and him in which they both voiced their remorse and grief. I saw this as a huge breakthrough. Behaviorally, Sammy also made great strides over the last few months of his commitment, learning how to manage anxiety through deep breathing and cognitive reframing. He also demonstrated an ability to control his aggression toward peers and model good leadership. When he was released from the facility, Sammy went to live with his mother and her boyfriend. This was not the best living situation for him because Sammy and his mother's boyfriend frequently fought. This man actually resented Sammy for taking up so much of mom's time and attention. . . . Unfortunately, Sammy started using drugs again and, while under the influence, he robbed a young boy of his bicycle. He was arrested and sent to a prison for young men. I was devastated. At first, it seemed like all our hard work was down the drain. Then I heard through the juvenile justice grapevine that Sammy was doing OK in prison . . . and when scared or stressed he was still practicing his deep breathing! It was then I decided that even though his was not what I would call a "success story," I had perhaps offered this young man some experiences and tools that would benefit him in the future. I have always wondered how Sammy's life turned out.

—*KFC*

Even when intensive training is not available to human service workers, mentoring can usually be accessed within their organizations. Mentoring is increasingly understood to be an important component of professional development in the field of social work. It involves an experienced worker helping a new or less experienced one learn new strategies for practice. The role of the mentor is to assist the mentee in developing a professional identity and in acquiring a particular set of competencies (Todd & Storm, 1997). Research has shown that mentors can have a huge influence on the learning of social workers (Bourn & Bootle, 2005; McGeorge & Carlson, 2010). They do so by modeling the use of important skills, thus providing vicarious experiences. They also relay confidence in their mentees' ability to master certain tasks (verbal persuasion). In addition, they provide immediate feedback concerning their mentees' performance in various types of work-related situations. Therefore, when we find a good mentor we have taken an important step toward building confidence and competence in our practice.

Effectiveness in social work is also furthered through a systematic approach to evaluating our interventions. Some authors have argued that the gathering of practice-based evidence is even more useful to community-based practitioners in determining service delivery choices than tightly controlled efficacy studies (Sexton & Douglas Kelley, 2010). When we integrate evaluation into our practice, we accumulate evidence concerning both our process and outcomes. Information about our process can be gathered by routinely asking for feedback from our clients or client systems about the strengths and limitations of our work with them. For example, we might ask our clients about the extent to which they are feeling heard and understood in our meetings together. Or we might ask for their views on "what's working and what's not working" as it relates to services provided. On the basis of this feedback, we may revise our approach to increase our clients' engagement in services and satisfaction with treatment. In this way, we are taking part in what DePoy and French Gilson (2003) referred to as *reflexive intervention,* a process of "looking inward" that is an "essential obligation of every social worker" (p. 12).

Outcomes identified for our practice-based evaluation should be client-centered, meaning that they matter to the individual, family, group, or community that we are striving to help. For instance, it is important that we track our clients' progress over time in reducing symptoms and overcoming problems or in achieving stated goals and objectives. If we find that good progress has been made in critical areas, this information provides an indication of competence that supports enactive mastery. On the other hand, if we discover that progress has not occurred, we may choose to change course. This shift in the focus of our intervention may improve our long-range, case-related outcomes and ultimate effectiveness.

Reader Reflections

After reading the questions for process assessment listed in Questions for Process Assessment, answer the following:

Questions for Process Assessment

Monitoring our process involves asking questions to obtain our clients' perspectives regarding the interventions that have been used, their strengths and limitations, and the areas needing improvement. Examples of questions that may be posed include the following:

- What occurred during our sessions/meetings together?
- What parts of the sessions/meetings were most helpful?
- Did you feel understood and treated with respect?
- Were your strengths identified and appreciated?
- Did we talk about what you wanted to discuss?
- What did I do that you would like to see continue?
- What did I do that should not continue?
- What discussions or activities helped you learn?
- What discussions or activities helped you reach your goals?
- Was there anything missing from our sessions/meetings?
- What changes would you like to see in our work together?

For additional resources supporting feedback-informed practice, see ICCE Web site: http://centerforclinicalexcellence.com.

1) What questions might you ask your clients or client systems to obtain feedback about your process of service delivery?
2) What information do you need to track your outcomes with clients or client systems?
3) How will you use this information to improve your self-efficacy?

Clearly, these processes for cultivating competence necessitate a willingness to accept a state of vulnerability as we acknowledge a need for change or self-improvement. Brown (2010), a social work scholar, conducted groundbreaking research that illuminates the importance of embracing vulnerability. On the basis of interviews conducted over a 10-year period, she provided insight on what it takes to participate in "wholehearted living," in which we "engage in our lives from a place of worthiness" (Brown, 2010, p.1). She acknowledged that we all struggle with shame as well as fear that we are not good enough. Such emotions hold us back from authentic and meaningful living. Brown (2010) further suggested that we can learn a great deal from people who have overcome these difficulties. These resilient individuals develop knowledge and claim power by being kind and gentle with themselves as they work to discover their own value and worth. They let go of worry about what other people think. They give up beliefs about who they think they are supposed to be. Instead, they embrace who they are—flaws, imperfections, and all.

One strategy that Brown (2010) shared for furthering wholehearted living is referred to as "digging deep." She made clear that she found the need to destroy her old "dig deep button" that was counterproductive. When activated, it prompted her to push through even when she was overwhelmed and when there was precious little time for self-care. She stated the following:

> You know the dig-deep button, right? It's the button that you rely on when you're too bone-tired to get up one more time in the middle of the night or to do one more load of throw-up-diarrhea laundry or to catch one more plane or to return one more phone call or to please/perform/ perfect the way you normally do even when you just want to flip someone off and hide under the covers. (Brown, 2010, p. 3)

On the basis of the approach of the resilient men and women in her research, Brown (2010) discovered a new version of digging deep that she found to be much more motivating when we are feeling depleted or down. It involves being deliberate in thoughts and actions, finding the inspiration to make new choices, taking action in a self-compassionate way, and restoring ourselves, as needed. Clearly, this type of orientation toward risk taking can help social workers striving to cultivate competence and actualize their potential.

Conclusion

When we think of ourselves as skilled and capable at what we do, we are better able to manage stress and maintain our commitment to a difficult yet rewarding career. Thus, self-efficacy is a critical component of self-care. There are a number of threats to perceived efficacy commonly seen in our profession, including irrational beliefs and faulty assumptions that contribute to feelings of inadequacy. It is important that workers examine their thinking and pay particular attention to patterns that pose such threats. Some may consider the adoption of one or more the strategies we feature in this chapter for combating these tendencies and sustaining self-efficacy in social work. As we noted in previous chapters, a kind and gentle approach to self-care is recommended, one that recognizes strengths, tolerates limitations, and embraces risk taking and vulnerability.

Questions for Discussion

1. Why is there not a fixed relationship between self-efficacy and self-esteem? What variables might mediate between the two?
2. What sociocultural forces encourage us to take on musturbations?
3. What are some goals commonly adopted in your field of practice that might be partialized into more manageable portions?
4. What are some process assessment questions that you might ask your clients?
5. In what situations are you required to "dig deep" in social work?

Chapter Exercises

1. Sources of Self-Efficacy

Consider the various sources self-efficacy discussed previously. Identify ways that you have acquired perceptions of competence in your life. How important has enactive mastery been relative to vicarious experiences, verbal persuasion or physiological/affective states? Give examples.

2. Threats to Your Self-Efficacy

Review the misguided beliefs discussed above and the faulty beliefs listed in *Replacing Thoughts that Threaten Self-Efficacy*. Are there times when you fall into these thinking patterns? If so, what replacement thoughts might work best for you?

3. Cultivating Competence

With permission from others involved, tape record (audio or video) a client session or group meeting in which you are taking a lead role. Then watch or listen to the tape. What thoughts or feelings come up for you?

Ask a trusted colleague or supervisor to observe you in a live or taped session and provide you with feedback. Reflect on the extent to which you feel vulnerable throughout this process? How are you managing your feelings associated with this form of risk taking?

PART III
Organizational Strategies for Self-Care

Chapter 6

Understanding Organizations and Our Fit within Them

written with Bob Steiner

Most social workers will spend much of their careers working in organizations. Some of the stress that they experience at work is because of their relationship with the organization. Learning to analyze and better understand how organizations work and how each of us functions within them, are important components of effective social work practice. These perspectives are also important in identifying causes of workplace stress and thinking about more effective self-care. This chapter focuses on helping the reader assess and analyze organizations from a number of vantage points. It also provides an opportunity for readers to analyze themselves in relation to their agencies and look for areas of fit and areas of mismatch. Some of the personal and organizational characteristics that are examined in this chapter are ones for which there are opportunities for change to improve fit and reduce stress. Others, such as vision and mission, are realities that are unlikely to change. Discovering that mismatch should offer readers some insight into what might be causing stress and the opportunity to consider whether the stress is manageable. If readers are not comfortable in their current agencies, this knowledge can offer ideas about what might be a better fit. Finally, the chapter discusses approaches to managing mismatch with the aim of reducing stress and burnout and improving effectiveness and satisfaction at work.

It is useful to note that an organizational analysis is a glimpse of an organization at one point in time, through one subjective perspective. Organizations are not static—what is true of an organization this week, might not be true in a year. In addition, each of us sees an organization through our own unique lens. Several people conducting the same analysis might draw very different conclusions. As we discuss in the following pages, an individual's lens is influenced by numerous factors. We must understand both the organization and ourselves to understand our experience within the organization. Throughout the chapter are questions to encourage you to think more deeply about your organization and about your experiences there.

Basics of Understanding Human Service Organizations

Vision and Mission

A central first step toward understanding an organization is to look at its vision and mission. Vision and mission statements define and guide an organization. A vision statement expresses the long-term change the organization would like to see through its work, helping people think about what is possible. It focuses on the big picture, describing the future people want to create for their community. The mission statement is more concrete, describing the approach the organization will take to make the vision a reality. For example, a housing organization might have the following vision and mission statements:

- The Vision of New World Housing is a community where all people have a safe, affordable, and healthy place to call home.
- The Mission of New World Housing is to bring community partners together to build safe and affordable housing and to advocate for community members who are facing eviction and foreclosure.

When beginning to understand fit in an organization, one can ask questions about its vision and mission and how these affect the work that the organization is doing. Are you a fit with the organization's mission and vision? Does the organization's vision and mission stir your passion, and do they fit with your view of how you want your community to be? Does the mission describe a process for creating change that fits with the approach you think works best or that best fits with the type of work you want to do?

Organizational Diversity

Organizations are complex systems structured in a variety of ways, using different management and leadership approaches. Within organizations, one can often see significant differences in the ways individual departments are managed. For example, there might be large differences in management approaches between the human resources department and the youth training division of a family services agency. Adding to this complexity are the vast differences we find among the administration and staff. People bring both visible differences to the workplace, such as their physical appearance, and invisible characteristics, such as their values and beliefs. It is important to be aware of all these aspects of difference as they can significantly affect how people interact with colleagues in the workplace.

With greater mobility in our society, increased immigration in recent decades, and more opportunities in the workplace for people with different backgrounds, diversity among staff has grown steadily. Statistics abound showing this dramatic change, as can be seen with the example of working women. The number of women in the workforce doubled from 1970 to 2010 and, in the same time period, the percentage of women with college degrees tripled from 11 percent to 36 percent. Over 70 percent of mothers with children under age 18 could be found in the workplace at the turn of the present century, compared with 47 percent in 1975 and fewer than 20 percent in 1950 (Cohany & Sok, 2007). Similar changes can be seen with generational diversity as baby boomers age or with cultural diversity in many parts of the country as new immigrants join the American workforce. One result of increased diversity is dynamic and complex work environments, with people challenged to work effectively despite differences among colleagues.

At the heart of working with difference is our bias toward other people. Many of us will deny that we have any bias; it is not something we are proud of or readily admit. But if we are honest, we see that we do indeed have biases. The tricky part of bias is that it can be conscious or unconscious, and we are often unaware of our perceptions and the effect they can have. Consider the ongoing research at Harvard University, designed to determine how pervasive social bias is by assessing the implicit biases of over 4.5 million people. That research found that people have negative associations with certain social groups, even if they genuinely feel they do not have negative biases. For example, more than 80 percent of respondents in this research had negative biases toward older adults as compared with younger adults, and nearly the same percentage of self-identified white or Asian respondents had more favorable biases toward European Americans as compared with African Americans (Harvard University, 2012).

Bias at work, which can be experienced at many levels in an organization, can affect how we interact with others and the decisions we make. For example, if a manager who is hiring for a certain position or is considering various candidates for promotion were raised in a culture that emphasizes a strong handshake, eye contact, and assertiveness, he or she might favor someone with those traits over a more technically qualified candidate whose culture emphasizes the importance of nonassertiveness or not making direct eye contact. Bias can be based on social identities, including race–ethnicity, class, religion, gender, sexual orientation, gender identity, ability status, and age. It can also be based on such aspects as how people dress, level of education, and social customs.

People's biases can lead them to favor certain traits over others that have nothing to do with ability or job performance. Differences can also lead to damaging organizational dynamics such as instances in which cliques or "in-groups" and "out-groups" are formed. When people are treated like outsiders, they can feel excluded and alienated and might be less effective in their work or even leave the agency.

Diversity in organizations has been a much discussed topic for several decades. The need for greater focus on diversity gained momentum as a result of the civil rights movement in the 1960s, during which time equal opportunity and antidiscrimination laws were passed to ensure that people were treated equitably in the workplace. Many organizations that initially increased diversity to meet legal requirements began to hire a diverse workforce as a moral obligation, and most recently, as a strategy to become more effective. Organizations have realized that to be most relevant, their staff and clients need to replicate the overall diversity found in society. Moreover, diversity has been shown to improve performance by bringing in varied perspectives, approaches, and insights for more effective problem solving (Page, 2007). If we are not open to differences and aware of our biases, we are less likely to reap the benefits that diversity can bring to organizations.

The historical challenge with this emphasis on diversity was that organizations consciously brought in different types of people but did not have an environment that embraced and supported that difference. It is increasingly clear that to support diversity, we must have inclusive environments that ensure that difference can thrive. Consequently, organizations must be aware of both diversity (the mix of people), and inclusion (the environment that allows this mix to succeed). Inclusion is explored in more depth in chapter 8.

Reader Reflections

1) Does your organization have policies that promote the diversity of staff and clients?

2) Can you see the biases of the organization's administration or of your coworkers in the policies and practices in the organization?

3) What biases do you have that might affect how you relate to others at work? What assumptions are your biases based on?

4) How are people treated relative to their differences?

5) Are there in-groups and out-groups that form as a result of differences? Do some people get included and others excluded?

Organizational Culture

> Sandra has been working in her new job for nearly a month and feels like she just doesn't fit in. Her supervisor and colleagues do things differently and seem to value aspects of work that she does not really identify with or understand. She can't put her finger on the exact problem, but she feels alienated, like an outsider.

What Sandra is experiencing is quite common among people starting new jobs or field placements. To a greater or lesser degree, people's values and ways of working can clash with those of their new organization. This clash or mismatch of culture and values can result in significant workplace challenges for both individuals and organizations. This can result in lower individual and organizational effectiveness and can also lead to burnout. As Maslach and Leiter (2005a) noted, "Burnout reflects an uneasy relationship between people and their work. Like relationship problems between two people, those between people and their work usually indicate a bad fit between the two, rather than *just* individual weaknesses, or *just* evil workplaces" (p. 44).

Having an increasingly diverse workforce can intensify cultural challenges. The word *culture* has many connotations, yet for our purposes, a good definition is "the set of shared attitudes, values, goals, and practices that characterizes an institution or organization" (Merriam-Webster, 2012). Organizations can have significantly different cultures. Compare the culture you see in a court, hospital, or large agency with that of a small nonprofit organization or a voluntary association. Even within an organization, certain departments or teams can have their own unique culture that differs from others in the same agency.

It is important to understand the dominant culture in an organization and how our individual culture might differ from it. Our experience of this difference can affect our relationships with others and ultimately our job satisfaction and ability to work effectively. It is also noteworthy that both individual and organizational cultures are driven by values. That is important to understand if the goal is to reduce the negative effects that a clash of culture can have on individuals and the organization. Take the example of an organization that emphasizes the importance of completing tasks and an employee who prefers to focus on relationships before getting down to the task at hand. The employee might believe that it is important to spend time getting to know colleagues and build relationships as part of task completion. This aspect of her culture might be driven by a core value of connecting with others as a prerequisite for building trust. This trust is seen as essential for effective working relationships. However, others in the organization might believe that this employee is wasting time. They might value merit, which means that building trust is based on completing tasks. The key is to understand how important and deeply embedded these core values are to each person. If we only consider the behaviors in an interaction, then our counterparts can seem either rude, shallow, or as wasting our time. Understanding someone's core values, on the other hand, allows us to see that there is a strategic, deep-seated reason for the behaviors exhibited. This can ultimately help us become more tolerant of differences, with a greater willingness to find ways to work together. This concept can be understood through the metaphor of an iceberg, as seen in Figure 1. The behaviors that we see on the surface, although important, do not tell the whole story.

Finding Your Fit

Understanding Organizational and Personal Culture

Part of what makes an organization complex (and arguably very interesting) are the myriad cultural differences found among the administrators, staff, and other stakeholders such as the board of directors and clients served. Organizational culture is often heavily influenced by the leadership, and in some agencies the culture can be quite strong. To work most effectively and manage stress, individuals must understand the organizational culture and how they can best navigate within it to facilitate greater alignment with differences.

There are many aspects of culture that one can identify within an organization. Researchers, psychologists, and anthropologists have determined a wide range of factors that comprise organizational culture (for example, Hall, 1983; Hofstede, 2001; House, Hanges, Javidan, Dorfman, & Gupin, 2004; Kluckhohn & Strodtbeck, 1961; Schmitz, 2006; Trompenaars & Hampden-Turner, 1998). There are several key distinctions commonly used that are helpful in understanding how one fits into the culture of an organization:

Figure 1: Our Values Drive Our Behavior

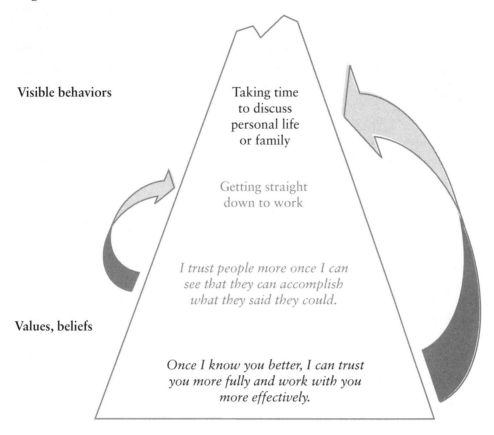

Visible behaviors

Taking time
to discuss
personal life
or family

Getting straight
down to work

*I trust people more once I can
see that they can accomplish
what they said they could.*

Values, beliefs

*Once I know you better, I can trust
you more fully and work with you
more effectively.*

- Degree of hierarchy
- Individualism
- Importance of relationships
- Directness in communication
- Perspective on time.

An additional cultural dimension, information processing and sharing, is less frequently discussed in the literature. It is, however, relevant to social work practice, so it is included here. Each of these dimensions is discussed in the following paragraphs. How to work with mismatch that might be producing stress is addressed in the last section of this chapter.

Degree of hierarchy. This aspect of culture reflects how important hierarchical structures and status are in an organization and how strongly its members adhere to an established chain of command. The more pronounced the distance between the top and bottom levels of an organization and the more deference people give to the different levels of power, authority, and status, the more hierarchical an organization is said to be. The distance between the top and the bottom levels of an organization can typically be seen in the following ways:

- The importance of formal titles and rank
- Variation in treatment (rights, power) for people at different levels
- Amount of interaction between different levels within the hierarchy
- Extent to which superiors tell staff what to do, versus consulting with them
- Amount of disagreement or questioning of superiors by staff members
- Adherence to hierarchical protocol or lines of authority

Effect of Differences

- Less hierarchical leaders might be seen as indecisive, lacking strong direction, or even weak, whereas their more hierarchical counterparts might come across as inflexible.
- More hierarchical staff members might seem to lack innovation or the courage to disagree, whereas less hierarchical colleagues might appear disrespectful of authority.
- Hierarchical colleagues might find people who do not use titles or acknowledge status to be disrespectful; less hierarchical people might find that their use creates distance.

Reader Reflections

1) How hierarchical is your organization?
2) What have you observed to make this determination?
3) What is your level of comfort with hierarchy or the lack of it, and how does that compare to the predominant culture in your organization?
4) Do you have a positive or negative experience in your organization with regard to the level of hierarchy? What are specific examples of how hierarchy (or the lack of it) affects you in your organization?

Individualism. This dimension looks at the degree to which organizations focus on the individual versus the community or the group. In organizations, do people identify themselves more as independent individuals or as parts of interdependent groups? Are people recognized and rewarded more for their individual achievements and contributions or for their collective efforts? What drives or motivates people to work as an individual or on a team?

The effects of an individualistic versus collectivistic perspective can be seen in areas such as how staff are motivated and rewarded, the design and allocation of work tasks, and the degree of consensus in decision making. An organizational focus on individualism or collectivism can also influence how well people collaborate with each other and how effectively they share information. Research has shown that team members from collectivistic cultures (those who identify with the group as opposed to an emphasis on the individual) can facilitate effective information sharing more readily than can those from individualistic cultures (Sarker, Nicholson, & Joshi, 2005).

This cultural category is assessed by the degree to which the organization

- focuses on the "I" versus the "we,"
- emphasizes independence among individuals versus interdependence,
- structures tasks and goals for individuals versus groups,
- recognizes and rewards individual versus group achievement,
- portrays organizational accomplishments as a team effort or highlights individual performance, and
- engages in group decision making for important issues.

Effects of Differences

- Individualists might feel they are not getting the individual recognition they would like, whereas others might perceive them as self-centered, and not committed to the group.
- Collectivists might be seen as lacking independence and individualists as lacking cooperation.
- Individualists might feel stressed working in groups, whereas their counterparts might become stressed due to a perceived lack of group cohesion, unity or purpose.

Reader Reflections

1) Is your organization more focused on the individual or the group?
2) Are people rewarded as teams, or more as individuals?
3) Do people primarily work alone or in groups?
4) How does this work environment compare to your preference and what is the impact on you of any difference?

Task versus relationship. Cultures can also be distinguished by the degree to which they emphasize relationships versus the accomplishment of tasks when working with others. This aspect of culture is readily apparent when we examine common interactions among staff. In task-focused cultures, people typically begin working with less socializing than is seen in more relationship-oriented cultures. This is not to say that task-oriented people do not socialize at work; they might just focus more on accomplishing a to-do list and then socialize after tasks have been completed. In contrast, relationship-focused people see building relationships as a precursor to accomplishing tasks. It is through a good relationship that they feel their best work is accomplished. Task-oriented people place trust in others once they see what another can accomplish. Those who place greater priority on relationships need the personal connection before extending trust.

As compared with most other countries in the world, the United States is an example of a culture in which the national tendency is to place greater emphasis on the accomplishment of tasks and achievements versus the importance of relationships in accomplishing those tasks. This national trend, however, appears to be changing with the influx of more relationship-oriented immigrant cultures into this country. The focus on task over relationship might also be less in some social work–related organizations because of the focus on relationships that exists in the profession. However, budget constraints and an emphasis placed on billable hours might push organizations to redirect their energies toward tasks and away from relationships.

This cultural dynamic manifests in the following ways:

- time spent on the job discussing nonwork topics,
- emphasis on achievements and goals versus building relationships,
- extent to which relationship and team building activities are used,
- a strict focus on agenda items in meetings versus social aspects of people's lives,
- knowledge of and focus on people's lives outside of work, and
- amount of socializing with colleagues inside and outside of the workplace.

Effects of Differences

- If relationship is more important to someone, they might find task-oriented colleagues to be unfriendly, cold, or not interested in their life, and mistrust them as a result.

- Task-oriented people might question their counterparts' seriousness about the job or their level of commitment to tasks or goals.
- Some might want more time to get to know people, whereas others find there is only time for the task, thus relationship should take a back seat.

Reader Reflections

1) Do you emphasize tasks or relationships more in your interactions with colleagues?
2) Is this behavior also your preference, or are you adapting to the norms of your organization?
3) Do you experience any challenges or frustrations around task versus relationship norms at work?

Directness in communication. When challenges arise, some people choose to address a conflict with another person head on, exhibiting a direct communication style. Others might opt to avoid a direct conflict and use more indirect or obscure language or even use a third party to convey their message. These differences in communication styles can not only cause misunderstandings, but also lead people to question others' intent and erode trust in the process. As we discussed earlier in the chapter, a person's communication style is driven by a value system that might be hidden. A direct communicator typically values expediency and clarity in communication and might feel that this directness and transparency in the short-term is best for long-term relationships. Indirect communicators, on the other hand, might see conflict as a detriment to long-term relationships. Their focus is on ensuring that people have harmonious interactions to support long-term relationships.

These communication style conflicts are often based on perceived intentions. Direct communicators might think indirect communicators are being dishonest or hiding something. Conversely, indirect communicators might experience their colleagues as overly abrasive or rude. The ability to see only the tip of the iceberg inhibits the development of trust and makes working relationships challenging. Identifying the core values underneath surface level behaviors might reveal that they come from good intentions, ideally lessening their negative effects. The differences in these communication styles manifest in the following behaviors:

- directly addressing difficult interpersonal topics with explicit language versus softening the conversation with implied verbal or nonverbal communication,

- using mediators or third parties as opposed to one-on-one resolution,
- pushing for immediate versus delayed conflict resolution, and
- relying on spoken versus written communication around conflict.

Effects of Differences

- Direct communicators often address conflict head on to move through it and into a better relationship; indirect communicators might talk around a conflict to preserve the relationship. Both can be concerned about the relationship but have differing beliefs about the best approach to maintaining it.
- Direct communicators might seem to be lacking in compassion, whereas indirect communicators might seem avoidant or confusing.
- Direct communicators believe that clarity and expediency create good and honest relationships, whereas indirect communicators think that an indirect path can help people save face and build strong and lasting relationships.

Reader Reflections

1) How direct are you in your communication with colleagues?
2) Is this level of directness your preferred way of communicating, or are you adapting to norms at work?
3) How direct is the communication of those with whom you work most closely? How comfortable are you with this level of directness?
4) What sort of challenges, if any, do you see with direct and indirect communication in your organization?

Perspective on time. Cultures often relate to time differently, which was studied extensively by Hall (1983). Hall labeled some cultures *monochronic* to reflect their focus on punctuality and doing a single thing at a time. He noted that others were *polychronic,* focusing on many things at a time and placing less importance on fixed timelines and schedules. This latter group typically feels that accomplishing the task at hand is more important than what they consider to be arbitrary confines of time. Many monochronic people feel that timeliness is both efficient and shows respect for others' time. Conversely, polychronic people tend to focus more on the quality of interactions or work output than on time parameters. For example, a polychronic person who is late for an engagement or meeting might stop to talk with a colleague he or she has not seen in some time. This might be particularly true if the person is more relationship-focused than task-oriented.

Doing many things at once, or multitasking, is a reality in most work-places. This is a challenge for monochronic people, who prefer to engage in fewer activities and have fewer interruptions than do people who are truly more polychronic. This variable relationship to time manifests in an organizational context in the following ways:

- degree of precision in starting and ending times for meetings,
- level of priority placed on quality of output and relationships versus timeliness,
- amount of interruption tolerated in interactions, and
- number of activities typically expected or conducted at any given time.

Effect of Differences

- Monochronic people might feel that interruptions and multiple demands shows disrespect for their time, versus their counterparts who might feel disrespected when attention is not given to the quality of interactions.
- Priorities can get questioned: is it more important to pay attention to punctuality and a single-focus on tasks, or to quality of life, output and relationships?
- Monochronic people might be viewed as rigid and inflexible, and polychromic people as disorganized and lacking focus.

Reader Reflections

1) Is it important to you to have something done on time, even if it is not done to your satisfaction? Would you rather take more time to finish something and hand it in late, knowing that it is up to your standards?
2) Which seems to be more valued in your organization? Are people penalized more for work not done well or work completed late?
3) Are you comfortable doing several things at once?
4) Is multitasking encouraged or even expected in your organization?
5) What sort of conflicts, if any, do you see between monochronic and polychronic people in your organization?

Information processing and sharing. Some individuals work through challenges by talking about them with friends and colleagues, whereas others tend to understand and solve problems on their own. The former can be thought of as external processors, and the latter as internal processors. Organizations can emphasize a culture that supports one or the other of these approaches. Some organizations encourage or even require staff to go to colleagues or supervisors when they are having challenges with a case or coworker. Staff in other agencies are discouraged from spending too much time processing what is going on for them. This difference was noted in our focus groups, as we discussed in chapter 3. Staff at several agencies described an open door policy, wherein they are encouraged to seek guidance and talk through challenges. As one focus group member stated, "Nobody is isolated. There is always the opportunity to call somebody and process. It is really helpful because the work is intense. There is never any judgment." Other respondents described being judged as weak or incapable of doing their jobs if they were in need of time for processing. Individuals who work most effectively by processing with others and who find themselves in an agency where this is frowned on can experience added stress and feel judged. Conversely, people who like to problem solve alone and work in agencies in which group processing is expected might feel challenged or overwhelmed with all of the discussion. Variations in information processing manifest in organizations in the following ways:

- the administration encourages or requires processing of difficult cases and/or regular supervision,
- supervision is primarily focused on productivity or billing, rather than on talking about cases and sharing feelings,
- staff members are judged for needing time to process or get assistance on difficult cases, and
- there is an open-door policy under which people can process or get help from their supervisor or others.

Effects of Differences

- External processors might be seen as weak for wanting or needing to talk about their feelings or talk through difficulties.
- Internal processors who feel overwhelmed with too much discussion might not be seen as team players; or if they are supervisors, they might be accused of not providing needed supervision.
- Supervisors who are internal processors might not see the need to talk about feelings or reflect on experiences to solve problems. They might be frustrated with their supervisees who want this type of supervision.

- External processors in internal processing environments might not have opportunities to talk through challenges and, thus, might not be as effective as others in solving problems.

Reader Reflections

1) Do you understand or resolve things better when you process them with others or on your own?
2) How do your colleagues, particularly those with whom you work closely, process information?
3) Is either approach better supported at your agency?
4) Do you experience any challenges or discomfort because of differences in this area?

Putting It All Together

Assessing and Managing Mismatch

To assess mismatch, take the time to answer the questions in the boxes throughout the chapter. This will provide an initial understanding of the structure and culture of your organization and of your preferences at work. If you are not certain about some of the answers, consider observing your own behaviors and those of colleagues and administrators. There are no right or wrong cultural traits, there are just similarities and differences that can result in a good fit or a mismatch. When mismatch occurs, it can cause discomfort or increased stress.

There are a variety of approaches to address mismatch and several things to consider before beginning the process. Mismatch could be present in several cultural dimensions, thus it would be difficult to address all of them at once. It is most beneficial to focus on one or two stressful areas at a time. When mismatch in one cultural dimension is having a large and negative effect, there are various ways to resolve the issues. The following approaches can be taken to reduce the negative impact of mismatch in any of the cultural dimensions.

- Gain a better understanding of the mismatch: That knowledge alone might begin to reduce stress. Sometimes knowing the causes of stress begins the process of reducing it.
- Consider your personal perspective concerning those who have different cultural values or behaviors. Be honest about biases: Starting from

an honest place, and being as nonjudgmental as possible, will make conversations about these issues more productive.

- On dimensions where you perceive differences between yourself and the dominant culture of the organization, identify specific behaviors that you have observed to support your perceptions. Think about how these behaviors have affected you. Consider what values and beliefs others might hold that are shaping their behaviors in this area. Consult *Values and Beliefs Underlying Various Cultural Dimensions* for a list of values and beliefs associated with the cultural orientations.

- Try to put yourself into another's shoes to understand what it would be like to hold those values and how you might behave if you did. Consider writing a sentence or two as that person. For example, if you are task-oriented and are having challenges with your counterpart, you might write, "As a relationship-oriented person, I really need to know people better so that I can trust them enough to work with them. This is really important to me and a prerequisite for productive interactions at work." By simply making that statement, it is easier to understand their world.

- Consider trying to modify your behavior to reduce mismatch. It is possible that a relatively small behavior change can alleviate tension or friction at work. If the change is not too difficult, a better working relationship might be worth compromising on a cultural preference.

- Talk to colleagues about concerns to determine whether others share them. If so, staff members might decide to work together to try to minimize areas of mismatch. In some cases, it might not be necessary for you to change your behavior to manage difference. Once your colleagues realize that mismatch is causing stress, they might be willing to alter their behavior.

- Approach those with power in the organization, usually supervisors or administrators, and determine where broader compromise might be possible. This last option is the riskiest, as those with more power might not be willing to share it or appreciate your concerns. Some individuals and organizations are more open to learning and change than are others. It is also important to recognize that agency administrators must consider what is best for all individual employees and the organization as a whole.

Values and Beliefs Underlying Various Cultural Dimensions

Cultural Orientation	Sample Core Values
More hierarchy	Clarity in roles, efficiency, respect, order
Less hierarchy	Autonomy, flexibility, creativity, openness
Individualism	Independence, being a "hero" for the group
Collectivism	Consensus, unity, teamwork
Relationship	Trust through knowing others
Task	Trust through merit
Direct communication	Clarity, expediency
Indirect communication	Harmony, saving face
Monochronic time	Respect for schedules
Polychronic time	Quality of output and relationships
Internal processing	Self-sufficiency, individual efforts
External processing	Increased input, group support

Understanding and assessing the organization's openness to change is important before approaching those in a formal leadership role. It is important to carefully think the issues through, devise a plan, and weigh the costs and benefits of this approach. Sometimes the risk to one's current job or future career might be too great to try to pursue change. Tips on having challenging conversations with supervisors and administrators are provided in *Tips for Challenging Conversations*. Remember that bridging cultural gaps is a negotiation, and a win–win outcome for individuals and the organization is the ultimate goal.

In the following paragraphs we offer suggestions for addressing mismatch on each of the six cultural dimensions discussed in this chapter. Suggestions for thinking, talking, and then acting on the issue are provided. This can help ensure that ideas have been thought out strategically, proposed in a way that will be well received by others, and acted on to effectively create change. Some of the suggestions offered might be more easily adopted than others. Trying to change behavior is often challenging. This is particularly true when the behavior is value driven. The extent to which you try to adopt behavioral suggestions will likely depend on how much the mismatch affects you.

Tips for Challenging Conversations

- Use "I," rather than "you" statements. For example, rather than saying "you are not providing the type of supervision I need," consider saying "I am someone who solves problems by talking them through. Would it be ok with you if we took some of our supervision time to talk through a difficult case?"
- Have a positive focus, stressing areas that are working well, before moving onto where there are challenges. When posing challenges, frame them as opportunities to optimize your collaboration.
- Acknowledge that there does not need to be perfect match for things to work well.
- Remember you are trying to resolve a challenge, rather than win an argument.
- If you have problems with a colleague or your supervisor, present facts that you have observed, rather than your interpretation of an issue. People tend to be more open to objective, factual observations than your interpretation of an event. For example, rather than saying "You weren't interested in my presentation (since you are not certain they were not interested), try saying, "I noticed you were texting on your phone while I was presenting." You can follow this up with how this behavior affected you so they know the impact of their behavior.
- Think about solutions that will be win/win, meaning they will work well for you, for your supervisor, for your colleagues, and for the organization. This might mean some compromise on all sides. Consider ways you might be able to compromise before you have the conversation. Be open to other possibilities while you are having the conversation.
- Ask your supervisor for his or her perspective on the issue, and really listen to what she or he has to say.
- Come prepared with some of your own ideas, rather than expecting your supervisor to fix the problem.

Addressing Hierarchy Mismatch

Possible course of action for more hierarchical people:

- Consider the advantages of open debate and disagreement in generating ideas and innovation that might come from a reduced emphasis on hierarchy and an increased focus on autonomy.
- If you usually tell supervisors or administrators what you think they want to hear, ask them if they are comfortable with you posing alternatives to their ideas.

- If you do not agree with something that is said, experiment with sharing your opinions and disagreement.
- After disagreeing, ask others how they perceived that interaction.
- Try being less formal in your language when addressing others, for example using titles less often if you are working with less hierarchical people.

Possible course of action for less hierarchical people:

- Try to appreciate the perspective that status and clear lines of authority bring efficiency and reduce uncertainty and chaos in an organization.
- Think strategically about how best to disagree with superiors; prioritize issues, and have conversations one-on-one so as not to threaten a superior's authority in a group.
- Talk to colleagues about the benefit of reduced hierarchy that can result in a broader sharing of ideas, which can lead to increased innovation.
- Consider being more formal in the way you address others, using titles if appropriate.

Addressing Individualism versus Collectivism Mismatch

Possible course of action for more individualistic people:

- Consider how a group can achieve more than individuals might be able to accomplish on their own.
- When looking at achievements, try to identify what the group has accomplished, rather than only what you have achieved.
- Proactively ask how you can support others at work and seek out opportunities to collaborate with colleagues.
- In meetings and other interactions with colleagues, try to use "we" to describe initiatives you're working on rather than using "I."

Possible course of action for more collectivistic people:

- Be aware of the needs that individualist colleagues might have to work alone and give them that space, if so desired.
- In meetings or other interactions with colleagues, highlight what individuals have accomplished.
- Focus on what you as an individual have accomplished, rather than solely identifying with what the group has achieved.

- If the predominant culture is individualistic, observe how much your colleagues work alone and try to do the same, consciously reducing the amount of your interaction, if that is the pattern you see.

Task versus Relationship Mismatch

Possible course of action for more relationship-oriented people:

- Be conscious of how your supervisor and colleagues act relative to tasks or small talk in meetings; try to undertake similar protocol in your interactions if possible.
- Talk to your colleagues about your desire for more connection and determine whether others have this same desire.
- During work hours, focus on tasks and goals first, and try to find other opportunities to get to know your colleagues at lunch or outside of work.
- Strong relationships might be important for you in trusting others. Try to consciously extend more trust toward others even if you do not know them as well as you would like.

Possible course of action for more task-oriented people:

- Try to understand the benefit of strong relationships at work, including the mutual trust that can be achieved between colleagues.
- Allocate a few minutes at the beginning of meetings to ask how people spent their weekend or what they are doing for upcoming holidays.
- If your "to do" list is important to you, put "get to know Mary better" as one of your tasks (you will feel like you have accomplished something important).
- Observe your colleagues: How much do they talk about their family, personal lives, or nonwork topics? Try and replicate those behaviors.

Directness in Communication

Possible course of action for more direct communicators:

- Observe how your colleagues handle disagreements or conflict, what language they use, and distinguish that from how you typically communicate.
- Talk to colleagues to understand how your communication style might be affecting them, and how it is being received.

- Proactively seek out coaching from colleagues about how you can communicate in a less direct way (get specific examples of less direct communication).
- Try to take some time before you react to someone with whom you disagree. Reflect on how you can respond in a less direct fashion.

Possible course of action for more indirect communicators:

- Think about your speech patterns, being aware of tenuous modifiers you might use, such as "sort of" or "kind of" and try to reduce the amount you use them. Observe the language your colleagues use and how it differs from yours.
- Talk with colleagues to determine whether they have issues with your communication style.
- Ask colleagues how you could communicate more directly; get specific examples where possible.
- Realize how direct communication in conflict situations might bring clarity to a situation and might be preferred to the indirect communication you consider more polite.

Perspective on Time

Possible course of action for monochronic people:

- Be aware of the importance polychronic people place on developing and maintaining relationships and producing quality outcomes over timeliness.
- Try to remember that people who multitask and are more comfortable with interruptions but share your goals of quality practice and excellence for clients just approach it differently.
- Discuss with colleagues your challenges with interruptions and multitasking and brainstorm ways that you can do your work one thing at a time with fewer interruptions, while they continue to do their work in ways that are best for them.
- When feeling stress from too many tasks to complete at once or ongoing interruptions, consider coping mechanisms that work for you, such as
  - focusing on the bigger picture of your goals, what you want to accomplish, and
  - centering yourself with deep, slow breathing.

Possible course of action for polychronic people:

- Be aware of the discomfort and stress that interruptions, tardiness, and a simultaneous focus on multiple activities can have on your monochronic coworkers.
- Consider how tardiness and the extension of meetings beyond predetermined timelines can adversely affect people's schedules.
- Ask colleagues to tell you how they experience your actions, which might include interruptions, multitasking, and not attending to deadlines.
- Make a habit of arriving at meetings early and preparing to end them on time.

Information Processing

Possible course of action for people who process internally:

- Pay attention to your thinking and notice the process you are going through to solve problems. Are there points in the process where you could share any of your thoughts with others? Can you see how problem solving with others might help you arrive at better solutions?
- Talk to colleagues about the process each of you uses to problem solve and to resolve difficult or emotionally charged situations. Try to understand how processing style might affect whether each of you has your needs met.
- Next time you are thinking through a problem or struggling with a case, find someone at work with whom you are comfortable and discuss what is going on.

Possible course of action for people who process externally:

- If you are not getting your processing needs met in the workplace, consider whether you have people in your life outside of work with whom you can discuss challenges.
- Talk to others at the agency. Try to find a colleague who also processes externally and with whom you can meet regularly to provide mutual peer support.
- Consider setting up group processing time with others who want it at the agency or with colleagues from other similar organizations.

As indicated, it is typically best to discuss differences with colleagues and supervisors and negotiate amicable strategies for all parties involved.

Conclusion

There are a variety of characteristics that make up an organization's culture, including those discussed in this chapter. It is important to recognize and understand where our organizations or programs fall on these cultural dimensions and our personal preferences with regard to them. This understanding allows agency staff members to note any areas of mismatch and assess how this mismatch might contribute to levels of stress on the job. A wide range of strategies can be used for addressing mismatch, some of which focus on observing the effects of differing work styles and preferences. Others involve modifying behavior and working toward compromise within the organization. When such efforts are applied broadly within a program, they might be part of a comprehensive approach to furthering the stress management and self-care of social workers.

Questions for Discussion

1. Does your organization have a written vision statement? Does it have a written mission statement? Discuss whether the two statements fit the descriptions of vision and mission statements given in this chapter. If not, discuss how they might be changed to be a better fit. Does the organization live up to its vision and mission statements?

2. Discuss the difference between diversity and inclusion. Why is each important?

3. Have you witnessed an occasion when you or someone else's biases shaped a hiring, promotion, or other personnel decision at an organization where you have worked? What effect did this have on the organization and the people involved?

4. Discuss your understanding of each of the six cultural dimensions presented in this chapter. Can you provide an example of a behavior that you believe illustrates each?

5. Try to describe the culture that exists in the organization where you are working or interning. Is the culture the same throughout the organization, or does it differ among departments? Do the strongest influences on the culture seem to be coming from administrators, from line staff, or from somewhere else?

Chapter Exercises

Representations of Culture

Choose an organization other than one where you are working or interning. You might consider your social work department or university if you are a student. Begin by looking at their Web site. If you can, also visit the organization. What do you see that you believe represents the organization's culture? Are there any indications of the organization's values or other indicators of culture, such as level or hierarchy or whether it is more of an individualistic or collectivist culture? Try to assess as many of the cultural dimensions as you can.

Comparing Perspectives

Interview several people at the agency where you work or are interning. Do they believe the organization or a program within the organization is hierarchical, individualistic or collectivistic, and more relationship or task-focused? Also ask them their perceptions of whether directness of communication is encouraged or supported in the organization and their perspective on whether the organization supports a monochronic or polychronic approach. Compare these perspectives to your own. If there are differences in perspective, what do you think might account for these?

Culture and Values

Spend some time with colleagues discussing your orientations as they relate to the cultural categories discussed in this chapter (hierarchy, individualism/collectivism, relationship vs. task focus, internal vs. external processing, perspective on time). Try to determine what values you hold that support each of these orientations. Discuss how understanding these values can help you resolve conflicts when they arise.

Chapter 7
Social Work Supervision

Consider yourself a novice social worker who recently started working at a public child welfare agency. One day, you are approached by one of the supervisors and directed to go out the front door of the office and climb into the back of an ambulance with two runaway adolescent girls. The girls' primary and more experienced workers are not available to provide support during transport to the hospital. Once in the ambulance, the first thing you notice is the strong stench of blood combined with body odor and semen. The girls are under the influence of methamphetamine, so their behavior is erratic and wild, yet you are able to piece together a story. They had been confined in a small apartment for the weekend, plied with drugs, and forced to have intercourse with two young men. Eventually, they had escaped and called for help. You accompany the girls to the hospital where they are shunned by nurses and provided with minimal medical care. When law enforcement officers arrive, they fail to take a report as they have had previous experience with the teens and believe that they are bringing these types of incidents on themselves. During the process of being taken by ambulance to another hospital for further evaluation, the girls manage to run away. When you return to the office, no one follows-up with you. Instead, you are left on your own to deal with the distress of your day. Days later, when your direct supervisor asks about this event, you deny your troubled emotions because you do not want to appear weak. You insist that you are "doing fine."

The incident described above illustrates supervision that may be well intended but misses the mark with regard to helping social workers cope with distressing circumstances on the job. It also speaks to the importance of a supervisory process that is rooted in a strong supervisory relationship and is responsive to the worker's need to process his or her reactions immediately following an upsetting event or crisis. In this chapter, we focus on the elements of high-quality supervision that play an important role in the management of social workers' morale within the agencies in which they work. In addition, we offer several supervisory strategies specifically intended to counteract *contagion*, or the spread of traumatic stress within social work organizations. A strength-based approach to clinical supervision is advocated that reinforces resilience and seeks out solutions, while contributing to the self-awareness, self-regulation, and self-efficacy of social workers. Finally, attention is devoted to methods for managing the stressors encountered by supervisors. Although it is expected that individuals with supervisory responsibilities will have a particular interest in these topics, the material to follow might also help interns or frontline workers in considering their needs for supervision. Ideally, the concepts presented in this chapter will spark conversation within programs and organizations about the ways in which supervision can be used to advance the self-care of all.

Quality Supervision

When done well, supervision in the profession of social work serves "administrative, educational, and supportive functions in interaction with the supervisee in the context of a positive relationship" (Kadushin, 1985, p. 24). It involves "a mutual sharing of questions, concerns, observations, and speculations to aid in selection of alternative techniques to apply in practice" (Munson, 2002, p. 11). According to Shulman (2010), high-quality supervision is a process that includes several phases: preliminary, beginning, middle, and ending. He suggested that the preliminary phase should begin before the first contact between the supervisor and the social worker. Here supervisors strive to "tune-in" to workers by sensitizing themselves to the thoughts and feelings that the latter may have as they enter the new supervisory relationship. The beginning phase should involve contracting that focuses on specifying the purpose of supervision, the supervisor's role, the needs of the supervisee, and mutual obligations. In the middle phase, effective supervisors use a variety of methods to support the supervisees' work with their clients or client systems. They use skills devoted to questioning, focused listening, and "reaching inside silences" (Shulman, 2010, p. 108). In addition, they show empathy, share information, explore taboo areas, and make requests for work in a caring manner. During the ending phase, the supervisor addresses themes and emotions concerning the worker's transition to a new supervisor or departure from the agency as a whole. The entire four-phase process is aimed at guiding social workers as they cope with the demands of various systems including clients, colleagues, agency administrators, and professionals from other organizations.

A wide body of research reinforces the importance of supervision in social work. Several studies have shown that inadequate supervisory support is a major factor contributing to high levels of turnover in the field of child welfare (Bernotavicz, 1997; Dickinson & Perry, 2002; Landsman, 2001; Rycraft, 1994; Samantrai, 1992). Other research has linked quality supervision to positive client outcomes, including satisfaction with services and goal attainment (Harkness, 1995; Harkness & Hensley, 1991; Kadushin & Harkness, 2002). Numerous studies have demonstrated a strong relationship between supportive supervision and the management of worker stress. For example, Kim and Lee (2009) examined the effects of different types of supervisory communication on stress among medical social workers. Their findings revealed that communication that is supportive and job relevant is related to lower levels of role strain and, consequently, less burnout. Mor Barak, Travis, Pyun, and Xie (2009) conducted a large meta-analysis that examined the effects of supervision on social workers across a variety of fields. Their results suggest that supervision that is focused on providing workers with task assistance, social and emotional support, and interpersonal interaction yields a variety of beneficial outcomes for supervisees, including job satisfaction and psychological well-being. These dimensions of supervision also reduce detrimental outcomes in workers, such as job stress and burnout.

The literature discusses various approaches to quality supervision that may be particularly effective in promoting the self-care of social workers. Shulman (2010) recommended an interactional approach that views supervision as a dynamic process in which the supervisor and worker continually influence one another through their behavior and expressed emotions. The development of a strong supervisory relationship is central to the effectiveness of this interactional process and is evident in the rapport, trust, and caring that is shared between supervisor and supervisee. Shulman (2010) also advocated the use of specific supervisory skills aimed at supporting workers in dealing with the obstacles they face on the job. For instance, supervisors are urged to "reach for feelings" in their supervisees when they appear stressed (p. 111). At times, this requires that the supervisor help the worker articulate emotions that he or she is having difficulty understanding or expressing. The supervisor is also encouraged to validate the feelings of the staff member, while avoiding a common tendency to rush in with false reassurances. This approach to supervision is intended to promote the self-awareness of social workers, especially as it relates to felt emotions. As we discussed in chapter 3, self-awareness is a key component of self-care.

Azar (2000) presented a cognitive–behavioral approach to supervision that is aimed at preventing burnout in child-maltreatment workers. In this approach, the supervisor identifies overly rigid expectations that the worker has about him- or herself, clients, or society. The supervisor then challenges these assumptions and attempts to replace them with more adaptive beliefs and interpretations. For example, the belief that "parents should want my help and view my efforts positively" might be reframed as "parents are often ambivalent about wanting help." The overall goal of this approach is to provide the practitioner with a "revised worldview that is more flexible and consonant with the realities of the work" (Azar, 2000, p. 651). This orientation helps workers enhance their self-awareness (by thinking about their thinking) and their self-regulation (by minding their mind).

Ellett (2009) suggested an approach to supervision that is based on Bandura's social-cognitive framework that we discussed in chapter 5. This approach seeks to strengthen the self-efficacy beliefs of social workers through close mentoring and continuous professional development. It promotes supervisee learning through modeling and other vicarious experiences, verbal persuasion that convinces them that they can be successful, and enactive mastery that is achieved when tasks are completed effectively (Pryce et al., 2007). For example, a worker that is learning how to prepare a court report might be offered an opportunity to shadow another worker as he is gathering all the needed information to complete one. Eventually newer social workers might be encouraged to conduct a report on their own, even when they are feeling a bit hesitant to do so. As they are preparing their first court documents, supervisees might be provided with on-going coaching and assistance until the final product is approved. This type of supervision may be especially helpful to novice workers who need task-focused support aimed at helping them maintain confidence, motivation, and persistence in the face of challenges and difficulties.

Some incorporate the principles of experiential learning into suggestions for social work supervisors. Kolb (1984) contended that experiential learning comprises four components: concrete experience, reflective observation, abstract conceptualization, and active experimentation. He further suggested that for complete learning to occur, individuals must move through all of four of these learning stages. Consistent with this theory, Raschick, Maypole, and Day (1998) recommended that social work supervisors and field educators tap the preferred learning modality of supervisees when structuring initial learning activities. Then they are encouraged to provide learning opportunities that target the three other stages. For example, the starting point for new workers who prefer learning through concrete experience might be to participate in a client interview with a more experienced worker. They might then be asked to reflect upon their experience. Next, they might be engaged in a discussion about the components of effective interviewing (*abstract conceptualization*) before they are expected to actively experiment with their new ideas about how to approach a client interview. By tailoring the process of supervision to the strengths and preferences of individual workers, supervisors expedite their acquisition of key competencies in social work.

Other scholars discuss the benefits of supervision that leverages group dynamics to advance the knowledge and skill of social workers. When conducting group supervision, supervisors facilitate group cohesion, constructive peer feedback, and the observational learning of supervisees (Linton & Hedstrom, 2006). Advantages to this modality include its cost effectiveness, along with the exposure of group members to varying perspectives. Furthermore, when psychological safety is established within the group, supervisees are empowered to take emotional risks and express vulnerability as they process case-related experiences (Fleming, Glass, Fujisaki, & Toner, 2010). Thus, group supervision holds the potential for promoting meaningful connections and mutual support between group members. As shown in earlier chapters, collegial support is a valuable tool for enhancing the self-care of social workers.

Finally, an ecological orientation toward supervision has been advanced that recognizes the need for change at both the individual and sociocultural levels (Gentile, Ballou, Roffman, & Ritchie, 2010). Here, the focus of supervision is expanded beyond casework and the clinical skills of the individual worker to include the interactions between that supervisee and his or her organizational environment. Consistent with this approach, supervisors may encourage employees to use the assessment tools discussed in chapter 6. Next, they might devote supervisory sessions to an examination of each worker's areas of fit or mismatch with the culture of the agency. Discussion can then focus on strategies for managing areas of mismatch. For example, if a social worker finds that he or she has a direct style of communicating that fits poorly with the indirect approach commonly used within the organization, the supervisor may suggest several activities. One might involve supervisee attending to the ways in which their directness affects others who communicate more indirectly. Another may involve their observation of coworkers to identify times when direct communication works well and when it does not. Conversations with colleagues might also be initiated to shed light on the advantages to both styles of interaction. When strategies such as these are carried out, the adaptability of the worker may be strengthened and supported.

Reader Reflections

1) Which of the previously noted approaches to supervision are most congruent with your supervisory style?
2) How might you adapt your approach to supervision so as to further promote the self-care of your social work supervisees?
3) What approach would be most beneficial to you as a supervisee?

Counteracting Contagion

A traumatic event experienced by one social worker can spread to influence others in an organization. This phenomenon has been referred to as the *spread effect* in which one worker's distress becomes contagious to other workers and their caseloads (Shulman, 2010, p. 309). It is more likely to occur when the organizational culture discourages workers from revealing their feelings of vulnerability and actually promotes the use of denial as an adaptive mechanism. The spread effect is also much more common within agencies where workers "have nowhere to turn to address the emotional feelings that the work brings up for them" (Pryce et al., 2007, p. 18). Thus, it is essential that supervisors make themselves available to their distressed workers and respond appropriately when they show signs of traumatic stress. Knowledge of crisis interventions that are successfully used for employee assistance is highly beneficial here.

One approach to helping practitioners cope with a crisis is called critical incident stress debriefing (CISD), otherwise known as traumatic event debriefing (TED). Bell (1995) described it as a structured group process that involves the following seven phases:

- Phase I: Introductions are made and rules are established.
- Phase II: Facts of the incident are discussed.

- Phase III: Initial thoughts at the time of the incident are identified.
- Phase IV: Emotional responses are explored.
- Phase V: Stress symptoms are normalized; strategies for harm reduction suggested.
- Phase VI: Participants socialize and prepare for reentry to the workplace.

Although research concerning the effectiveness of this strategy has produced mixed results (Robbins, 2002), CISD has been used successfully with emergency service workers who have witnessed a disaster. It is also being used across a wide range of incidents involving trauma. Pryce and colleagues (2010) recommended that child welfare agencies include CISD as part of their standard operating procedures in response to traumatic events. They cautioned, however, that it should not be used without adequate preparation and that facilitators of the process must be properly trained. Moreover, they advised that attendance at debriefing sessions be made optional as opposed to compulsory. Some individuals might be further traumatized if forced to attend against their own better judgment. If workers do not feel safe with and trusting of other group members, their participation is likely to be counterproductive.

As an alternative to the structured group approach to debriefing, supervisors might use elements of this model in providing a less formal and individual approach to crisis intervention with their supervisees. In doing so, however, they must respond quickly to their workers following a traumatizing incident. Next, they might ask for the facts of the event, from the perspective of the employee. Initial thoughts and perceptions that occurred for the supervisee could be identified. The emotions of the worker might be elicited, while he or she is provided an opportunity to vent about what was, for him or her, the most difficult part of the incident. Throughout this process, employee's stress reactions should be acknowledged and understood. Next, discussion might center on ways that the worker can manage the distress and carry on with responsibilities. If time off is needed, this should most definitely be granted. Finally, the supervisor should always remember to follow-up with the staff member when they are back on duty to ensure that they have recovered adequately from the traumatic event.

Also important, and rarely recognized, is the practice of preliminary briefing with supervisees. This approach assumes that the most attentive supervisors are the ones who anticipate the stress reactions of their workers prior to their involvement with complex cases and potentially trying activities.

When stress is seen as likely, the supervisor engages their staff member in discussion about how they might handle particular difficulties or challenging circumstances, should they occur. This supervisory strategy enhances the use of proactive coping of workers that was discussed in chapter 2. Proactive coping involves a process of considering predicable stressors, surmising one's likely appraisal of such events, and exploring possible courses of action in response. When employees are encouraged to use this form of coping, they are less likely to suffer from high levels of traumatic stress that can bleed over and negatively affect colleagues and coworkers.

Reader Reflections

1) How attentive is your agency to the briefing or debriefing needs of its workers?
2) How might you incorporate elements of the CISD model into your supervisory meetings with workers who have recently endured a client crisis?
3) What characteristics would you look for in a worker that might indicate that he or she is a good candidate for preliminary briefing?

Supporting Strengths and Solutions

All of the previously mentioned approaches to supervision are most beneficial to the self-care of social workers when they are used within the context of a strengths perspective. When applied to supervision, a strengths-based orientation promotes mutuality and partnership between the supervisor and the worker and "respectful give-and-take communication" (Lietz & Rounds, 2009, p. 129). It also provides a strengths-focused model of interaction for supervisees, which may guide their approach to clinical practice. When applied to casework, this model assists the practitioners in identifying and building on the assets of their clients, as they work toward resolving presenting problems. Strengths-based approaches to direct service and supervision are highly congruent with the mission of social work and the ethical principle that values respect for the inherent dignity and worth of the person.

Cohen (1999) contrasted strengths-based supervision with a more traditional, problem-centered approach that is said to produce anxiety in the supervisee. He stated the following:

> Supervisors can create a more supportive, less threatening environment for supervising strengths-oriented workers by defining the central

From the Field: To Brief and Debrief

When I was asked to be an agency field instructor to social work interns, I was honored and wanted to make sure I did the job well. Child welfare is a tough field and I wanted interns to feel supported. I knew that this would primarily happen through supervision. I was given some guidelines about how that was to look, but the specifics were vague. I took this as an opportunity to be creative. This is especially true when I was working with Samantha, a social work intern.

Early on, it became very clear that scheduled, weekly meetings were not the only venue for supervision. Certainly, Samantha and I valued that time together. However, it did not always meet our needs. Samantha was an eager intern, ready to face any situation. She was a "jump in and do it" kind of woman. As such, she was rarely going to voice worries or concerns about an assigned task, for fear it might make her look unwilling or incapable of getting the job done. This, to me, seemed problematic. If she could not express what she was really feeling, how would she be prepared? What we soon discovered was that it was problematic. Samantha shadowed a social worker on a child sexual abuse interview and had not accurately anticipated what would take place—both in the interview and in her. We debriefed for over an hour, yet neither of us felt better.

The next time Samantha was tasked to participate in a challenging situation with a family, in the field and without me tagging along, we scheduled a debriefing time for when she returned. But we also huddled for a pre-event meeting to help eliminate uneasiness and prevent stressful reactions. We shared ideas about what might happen, what a good experience might look like, and what we were worried about. We labeled our gut reactions, our objective versus subjective thoughts on the situation, and discussed what appeared to be working within the family. We talked about safety, emotions, fears, and hopes. From beginning to end, it was about a seven-minute conversation. And truthfully, it made the situation seem far less daunting.

When Samantha returned, we debriefed. It was quick and easy. She admitted that she had felt more prepared and confident in her skills for this situation and, as a result, better attended to the needs of the family. So why had we just been focusing on the debrief? Why not try to prevent stress or trauma? We decided in that moment that the pre-event meeting was extremely useful and was a needed addition to our regular supervision. We continued with this format: pre-event staff meetings, debriefing, and routine weekly supervision. While the challenges of her experiences increased, our pre-event and debriefing process time decreased. By the end of the year, Samantha continued to demonstrate ability, but she had also developed strong insight, awareness, and self-care. In addition, we both discovered the importance of prevention, not just with the families we serve, but also within our own practice.

—*MKM*

content of the supervisory session as a joint evaluation of the worker's recent successes rather than a joint struggle with questions, problems, and frustrations. (Cohen, 1999, p. 462)

Cohen (1999) also suggested that what is learned from a discussion of worker successes can then be applied to other more challenging situations and cases. When the overall focus of supervisory sessions is transformed in this manner, supervisees who seem "stuck" are helped to "pinpoint the strengths necessary to get the process moving again" (Cohen, 1999, p. 463). This approach is also credited for assisting social workers in overcoming the feelings of frustration and impotence that are often elicited by work with distressed and oppressed populations.

One version of strengths-based supervision that has received recent attention is rooted in a solution-focused framework. In their book, *Building Solutions in Child Protective Services,* Berg and Kelly (2000) discussed the application of solution-focused practice principles to the supervision and training of social workers. They encouraged supervisors to "lead from one step behind" so as to minimize hierarchical differences between the worker and themselves (p. 216). This entails taking a collaborative stance as opposed to an authoritative one in relation to supervisees. Supervisors are also urged to model solution-focused techniques for workers by

- using positive speech, such as agreeing with and praising the worker;
- implying advise rather than giving it directly;
- focusing advise on the client rather than the worker;
- mitigating advice by avoiding words such as "should" and "must;"
- replacing directives with observations;
- providing positive evaluations of the worker and teaching curiosity;
- using constructive as opposed to definitive dialogue; and
- using scaling and relationship questions.

Through the use of these methods, supervisors shift from searching for mistakes and telling workers where they are in error and what they should do. Instead, they ask questions to promote supervisees' curiosity about themselves and the clients they serve. They also strive to take the worker's perspective, while gently guiding them to consider other viewpoints. *Solution-Focused Techniques* provides illustrations of the use of these various solution-focused supervisory techniques.

Solution-Focused Techniques

Berg and Kelly (2000) suggested the following techniques for effective solution-focused supervision:

(1) Using positive speech
    "This case would be challenging for anyone"
    "How did you manage to get as far as you did?"
(2) Implying advice rather than giving it
    "What do you suppose might happen if you . . . "
    "It might be helpful if you . . . "
(3) Focusing advice on the client rather than the worker
    "It sounds like this client needs to . . . "
    "Perhaps this client would benefit by . . . "
(4) Mitigating advise by avoiding "should" or "must"
    "You might consider . . . "
    "I don't see any harm in . . ."
(5) Avoiding directives, replacing them with observations
    "It is interesting that this client seems to be asking for . . . "
    "What do you make of that?"
(6) Providing positive evaluations of the worker and teaching curiosity
    "I am sure you had a good reason for doing this"
    "What does this client want from you?"
(7) Modeling the use of constructive dialogue rather than definitive dialogue
    "What do you suppose they mean when they say . . . ?"
    "It is not unusual for clients to . . . "
(8) Using scaling and relationship questions
    "On a scale of 1 to 10, how safe is this client?"
    "What would this client say about her level of comfort with you?"
    (pp. 222–223)

The solution-focused approach to supervision is well suited to a focus on the self-care of social workers. For instance, a supervisor might periodically ask a scaling question to assess the stress level of his or her supervisee: "On a scale of 1 to 10, how stressed do you feel today?" The supervisor might then follow up with another question intended to elicit a solution: "What would you need in order to move two points lower on your stress scale?" The supervisor might also use positive speech by praising his or her supervisee's work: "Considering how tough this case is, you have accomplished a lot."

Or the supervisor might acknowledge the worker's persistence in the face of challenge: "How did you survive that dreadful home visit?" He or she might even imply advice rather than giving it: "I wonder if you would feel less overwhelmed if you asked for help from the case aid...any thoughts about that?" Finally, if a worker admits to feelings of disgust toward a particular client, the supervisor might prompt curiosity by asking: "What would we have to know about this person for his/her behavior to make sense?" Such comments and questions can assist distressed workers in overcoming a pessimistic perspective and in maintaining a focus on the potential of their clients, their work, and themselves as developing professionals.

Evaluating Supervision

Just as social workers have an obligation to evaluate the effectiveness of their practice, supervisors have a responsibility to evaluate the strengths and limitations of the supervision they provide. This can be approached in a variety of ways. For instance, supervisors can monitor the progress of their supervisees toward agreed upon learning or performance objectives. To do so, they might observe the worker in client sessions or case staffing sessions and assess the extent to which they demonstrate increased competence in the use of a particular skill set. Or they might review recorded interviews to determine the level of skill acquisition. Another approach to evaluation involves surveying workers about their perceptions concerning the quality of supervision. Milne and Reiser (2008) suggested the use of a questionnaire intended to assess the supervisees' satisfaction with supervision in the following domains:

- Frequency of meetings
- Duration of meetings
- Normative functions (assistance in planning and problem solving)
- Supportive functions (acceptance and recognition)
- Formative functions (assistance in becoming self-aware, seeing things more clearly)

A questionnaire of this kind could easily be developed and adapted to the supervisory needs within any social work organization.

Equally, if not more important, is the use of supervision time to talk openly about the supervisory process. It is essential that supervisors model receptivity to feedback about the work they are doing. This can be accomplished by periodically checking in with supervisees about the extent to

From the Field: Humor Helps

It was a dark and stormy February morning on a busy five-lane highway in south Sacramento. I was weaving in and out of traffic at 80 mph in the pouring rain to make up time. I was running late to do an intake with a patient named Amelia. When I finally arrived at the skilled-nursing facility (25 minutes late) where Amelia lived, I tried to simultaneously organize the intake paperwork and review her medical records as I ran to the building in the pouring rain. The patient's son, Jim, met me in the lobby and told me "She's having a bad day. She keeps saying she just wants to die." A client I had seen earlier in the day had disclosed suicidal ideations, so when I heard this from Jim I just thought to myself, "It's going to be one of those days." I followed him to Amelia's room where I found her lying in bed, her daughter-in-law sitting right beside her. I put my things down and kneeled by her bed. My face was no more than three inches from hers. She reached out her hand, and I held it between both of my hands; she intertwined her fingers with mine. Amelia then said "I just want to die." I asked her why she wanted to die. Was she in pain? Was living just getting too hard? She again responded, "I just want to die." While I was thinking of how to respond to this statement, I felt her body go limp. I looked at her and she had stopped breathing. I immediately felt bad that she had died without me being able to respond to her statement. I looked at the family who was watching me intensely and waiting for me to do something. The daughter-in-law began to wail and threw herself over Amelia's body. Jim sat quietly with tears rolling down his cheeks, staring down at the floor. I pressed the "call nurse" button and brushed the hair off of Amelia's face. I was trying to buy myself some time as I developed a plan to comfort and support the family through this moment. I gently placed her hand at her side and leaned over to push myself up with the help of her bed. As I leaned over Amelia unexpectedly yelled, "BAAAHH!!!!" I screamed and jumped; I thought she had died!

The next day in supervision, through bursts of laughter, I told my supervisor about this incident. He laughed along with me. Then he acknowledged that even though we were laughing about this situation, it must have been a scary thing for me to go through. He told me that he understood that it's hard enough to have someone repeatedly tell you they want to die, but to have them "die" without being able to respond to their statement is difficult. We spoke about how this prank might have helped her with her own death and dying issues. Up until this point, I had only been thinking about how it had affected me. At the end of supervision, I came to the conclusion that even though the situation was upsetting, it was really good practice for me. I had never been alone with anyone at the point of death before. We talked about how a lot of my fear in the situation came from my not knowing what to do. As I look back on this meeting with my supervisor, I appreciate his willingness to use humor in the moment to help me destress. He also validated my feelings about Amelia's fake death, and this helped me feel better about the incident. No matter where my social work journey takes me, I will always remember how to respond when someone dies . . . make sure they are really dead!

—*Christine*

which supervisory consultations are meeting their needs. In doing so, the supervisor provides staff members with a voice in shaping the process of supervision. This is likely to result in a greater supervisee investment. When feedback about supervision is positive, this may enhance the self-efficacy beliefs of the supervisor. When constructive criticism is offered, the supervisor may choose to adjust the focus of supervision in the manner suggested. Supervisors might use this type of process evaluation to ascertain the degree to which workers believe that supervision is serving to support their self-care. Such information might trigger a shift in the supervisors' approach that strengthens their overall contribution to the healthy functioning and well-being of their supervisees.

Supervisor Stress

Social work supervisors are certainly not immune to high levels of occupational stress. They have a great deal of responsibility that spans the monitoring of worker compliance with policies and procedures, the effectiveness of services delivered, and the functioning and well-being of supervisees. As a result of their role as "middle managers," they often feel caught between both the staff and the administration. This is especially problematic in work settings in which an "us-versus-them" attitude has been perpetuated between line employees and administrators (Shulman, 2010). To address this challenge, supervisors need to act as a "third force" or buffer against the complexity of the system (Shulman, 2010). They must also find ways to avoid taking sides with employees or administration and support both, as needed and appropriate. This can be a very difficult line to walk.

A special challenge occurs for supervisors who carry administrative responsibilities in addition to supervisory ones. When this is the case, it is not uncommon for administrative items (productivity reports, agency policies) to take center stage during supervisory sessions, thus limiting time devoted to cases, clinical skill development, and the exploration of worker stress or struggles with countertransference. This can result in supervisees being less satisfied with supervision. Supervisors may pick up on this dissatisfaction, which can intensify their own feelings of frustration about having to juggle multiple roles. One way to mitigate this problem is to create a structured agenda for supervisory meetings, with a strict limit placed on the amount of time devoted to administrative issues. A firm commitment might be made to preserve the rest of the meeting time for discussion related to cases and worker challenges or needs.

Supervisors are also called upon to mediate conflict between employees. In addition, they may need to manage conflict when it erupts between themselves and their supervisees. Misunderstandings and disagreements are common in social work organizations, and the process of resolving them is often emotionally charged. Korinek and Kimball (2003) recommended a collaborative approach to conflict resolution that creates a win–win result for both parties involved, as opposed to a winner and a loser. This process includes the following six steps:

1. Identifying the problem and unmet needs
2. Setting a date to discuss the issues
3. Describing the problem and unmet needs from each person's perspective
4. Considering the other person's point of view
5. Negotiating a solution
6. Following up on the implementation of the solution.

When the steps of this process are carefully followed, a meaningful solution is more likely to be reached. Consequently, emotions will be regulated and stress reactions contained.

Another stressor for social work supervisors involves their exposure to the pain of both their supervisees and the clients served by the organization. Within the context of supervision, social workers may disclose the troubling emotions that they experience as a result of dealing with client suffering. They may also present the details of client trauma, as encountered by individuals on their caseload. In response, supervisors may feel pressured to produce answers to complex situations that involve long-standing client difficulties associated with trauma, violence, addiction, and abuse. They may also find themselves caught up in heart wrenching accounts of client loss, sorrow, and misery. As a result, they may experience their own stress reactions and symptoms of secondary traumatic stress.

When distressed, it is vitally important that supervisors resist the temptation to seek relief through the staff that they supervise (Munson, 2002). To be effective, supervisors must maintain professional boundaries and avoid burdening supervisees with their own job-related struggles. Supervisors do, however, need a place where they can vent their emotions and process supervisory challenges. Peer support groups for supervisors are suggested to meet this need (Pryce et al., 2007). Supervision groups and collective training sessions for supervisors may also serve this purpose and are receiving increased attention in the literature. Collins-Camargo and Miller (2010) evaluated the effect of small group learning labs provided to frontline supervisors in four child welfare agencies. One benefit of the project that was clearly identified by study participants related to the creation of a forum for peer consultation and support. The use of this forum provided supervisors with a "sounding board" and someone to talk to about issues that they had previously kept to themselves (Pryce et al., p. 95). This appeared to reduce the isolation of supervisors and to prompt the sharing of resources across teams. Supervisors across all types of social work agencies need to be provided opportunities of this kind. By supporting supervisors, agencies support social workers and the clients they serve.

Reader Reflections

1) What aspect of the supervisory role do you find to be most challenging?
2) What support do you need to manage the stress involved with social work supervision?
3) Would the supervisors in your agency benefit by a peer support group?

Conclusion

Social work supervisors play a pivotal role in the management of stress within an organization. Thus, it is important that they receive training in the use of one or more quality approaches to supervision. They also need to acquire skill in proactive briefing and debriefing as a means of managing worker reactions to critical or traumatizing incidents. When supervisors are prepared to embrace an overall orientation toward supervision that is strengths-based and solution-focused, they are best equipped to strengthen and support employees. It is important to recognize, however, that the job of the supervisor carries its own inherent stressors. Supervisors need their own support to advance their self-care, as well as that of their supervisees.

Questions for Discussion

7. How do you go about "tuning in" to your supervisees? What evidence do you have that your supervisor has "tuned in" to you?
8. In what ways has the "spread effect" affected your agency?
9. To what extent is your approach to supervision strength-based? How might you increase your focus on supervisee strengths and solutions?
10.   Are you sometimes tempted to share your stories of work-related woe with your supervisees? How do you deal with that temptation?
11.   What are your sources of support as a supervisor?

Chapter Exercises

1. Briefing and Debriefing
Design a protocol for preliminary briefing and debriefing for your agency. When would they be used? How would an employee access this type of support? Who would provide the service? How might you justify the need for these interventions?

2. Strengths-Based Supervision
After obtaining consent from your supervisee, record (audio or video) a supervisory session. Next, play back the recording. Note the comments you made and the questions you asked that were strength-based or solution-focused. Also note times when you might have used these techniques to further support your supervisee.

3. Peer Support for Supervisors
Talk to the other supervisors in your agency about the potential benefits of a peer support group for those carrying supervisory responsibilities. If they are in favor, present this information to your administration. Discuss the ways in which such a group might enhance the functioning of supervisors. Also consider barriers that might possibly interfere with consistent participation. How might these barriers be managed?

Chapter 8
Workplace Wellness

In a 2011 national poll conducted by the American Psychological Association (APA), 36 percent of workers reported experiencing significant work stress regularly. The same poll found that 43 percent of employees were concerned about a heavy workload, 40 percent were worried about unrealistic job expectations, and 39 percent cited long hours as a source of stress (APA, 2011). These data suggest that organizational approaches to stress management are needed to supplement the individual approaches that were suggested in earlier chapters. Although individual efforts are clearly necessary, they are likely not enough. None of the concerns noted in the APA poll can be effectively addressed by personal strategies devoted to self-care. Thus, in addition to the efforts made by individual employees, it is important for organizations to take broader, structural steps to reduce employee stress and create workplace wellness.

Reducing Workplace Stressors through Organizational Change

Organizational changes that are implemented to reduce stress benefit not only individual staff members, but also clients and the organization as a whole. Organizations pay a significant price for high levels of employee stress. Stress is estimated to cost U.S. workplaces roughly $300 billion a year as a result of absenteeism, health care expenses, turnover, workers' compensation awards, and reduced productivity (Schwartz, 2004). It is also estimated that up to 60 percent of workers' compensation, 10 percent of medical prescription, and 40 percent of turnover costs are the result of stress in the workplace (Tangri, 2003). In environments in which employees feel stressed and unsafe, they are less likely to take risks and be innovative or to speak up when there are problems (Edmonson, 2002). There is growing evidence that organizations that take the initiative to create healthier, lower stress workplaces are rewarded in a variety of ways. For example, eight organizations that have been recognized for their outstanding work in creating a healthy work environment report benefits in several key areas, including the following:

- Reduced turnover (an average rate of 11%, as compared with the national average of 38%)
- Reduced percentage of employees reporting chronic work stress (18% , as compared with 36% nationally)
- Increased percentage of workers reporting job satisfaction (87%, as compared with 69% in the general population). (APA, 2011)

There are many approaches to making changes in the workplace that can help reduce stress, encourage self-care, and improve morale. There is not one approach that will work for all organizations. One way to begin to determine which changes will be most effective is to learn about what is causing stress in the workplace. One approach to understanding specific stressors is to survey employees to determine what the largest sources of stress are for them on the job. Efforts can then be implemented to address these specific challenges. This chapter examines three approaches to reducing workplace stress and creating a healthier work environment. The three approaches are supporting psychological health and safety, incorporating inclusion, and valuing vision.

The intended audience includes current managers and administrators, as well as direct service employees who can suggest organizational changes. It is hoped that workers at all levels of the social work organization will have opportunities to participate in the development and implementation of practices, programs, and policies that support self-care.

Supporting Psychological Health and Safety

One area that is important in addressing stress and self-care in the workplace is *psychological safety*. The concept of psychological safety at work is relatively new. Physical risks at work have long been addressed through federal and state regulations, but psychological danger has not. This is beginning to change. Some laws have been passed that address specific issues of psychological safety, including laws against harassment in the workplace. Several European countries have passed legislation that addresses a broader range of psychosocial causes of stress at work (Ertel, Stilijanow, Cvitkovic, & Lenhardt, 2008). The Canadian government recently launched an effort to develop national standards for employers to follow to protect workers from psychological harm and to promote psychological well-being (Saint-Cyr, 2011). They note that mental illness costs Canada roughly $51 billion a year and that workplace losses account for about $20 billion of that. Psychologically safer and healthier workplaces would seem to benefit the government, employers, and employees. Although it has not been addressed at a national level in the United States, increasing attention is being paid to psychological health in work settings in some sectors. APA has been studying stress and psychological health and now gives out an award each year to honor employers who have created a psychologically healthy workplace (APA, 2011). In addition, the Center for the Promotion of Health in the New England Workplace was founded in 2006 to address health issues related to work, with a major focus on stress and psychological health.

Psychologist David Ballard defines a psychologically healthy workplace as one that is "committed to fostering employee health and well-being while enhancing organizational performance and productivity" (Mullin, 2005). This suggests that there is a joint focus on employee well-being and achieving the mission of the organization. Another way of understanding a psychologically safe workplace is that it is one that is conducive to supporting or sustaining employee psychological health. Psychological health is a concept that has been widely discussed by researchers and practitioners for years. As Boudrias and colleagues (2011) noted, psychological health refers both to the presence of positive affective states a person exhibits (well-being) and an absence of negative symptoms (distress). It includes whether a person is able to cope with what comes up in life and is generally happy. Happiness comes and goes, but people in good psychological health tend to have an overall positive mood. Another view of psychological health concerns our connections with others. People who have strong relationships with friends, family, and coworkers are thought to be more psychologically healthy. Finally, psychological health can refer to whether or not people feel calm and peaceful most of the time. Carried into the workplace, this concept of psychological health can be seen as encompassing the extent to which people generally feel peaceful, connected to others, relatively free from distress, and satisfied.

Whether someone feels psychologically safe at work depends on a number of factors, including personal resources, job demands, and social and organizational resources (Boudrias et al., 2011). Previous chapters examine the personal resources that individuals bring to the workplace, including self-awareness, self-regulation, and self-efficacy. Such resources are likely to help workers maintain a sense of psychological safety, even when circumstances are challenging. In addition to supporting these individual approaches to well-being at work, organizations can develop policies and practices that address issues of job demands and social and organizational resources that are available to employees. What they implement can result in psychologically safe workplaces or workplaces in which people feel threatened and distressed.

Reader Reflection

1) What personal resources do you bring to work that contribute to your feeling more peace and less distress in your work life?
2) What workplace policies or practices contribute to your feeling more happiness and less distress at work?
3) What workplace policies or practices contribute to increased stress and distress for you?

Growing out of the concept of psychological safety is psychological safety climate theory. Unlike other theories about work stress, psychological safety climate theory suggests that workplace stress is not so much an individual problem because "the origins of stress are further upstream (more at the organizational level); it [this theory] focuses on safe place over safe person" (Idris, Dollard, Coward, & Dormann, 2012, pp. 19–20). Because many theories about workplace stress focus on individual problems that lead to stress, the solutions that grow from them are often individual-oriented solutions. We have noted throughout this book that individuals must take some responsibility for being aware of their stress and taking steps to engage in self-care. However, psychological safety climate theory reminds us that this is not enough to truly address the epidemic of stress that we face. If much of the origins of stress are actually at the organizational level, then effective actions to reduce stress must be aimed at changes in both the organization and the individual.

Having our primary psychological needs met can contribute to feelings of psychological safety. In their self-determination theory, Deci and Ryan (2000) proposed that people have three innate psychological needs that play a large role in determining their motivations and whether they reach their goals. Their research has been used to assess and improve psychological health and safety in a variety of work settings. The three needs they noted are the need for *autonomy, competence,* and *relatedness.* Autonomy refers to the need to be true to our self and to direct our own path. They note that autonomy does not mean being independent of others. Competence speaks to our need to be effective in what we do. Relatedness refers to the connections we make with other people and whether we feel a sense of inclusion and belonging. As Deci and Ryan (2000) noted, "(T)he presence versus absence of environmental conditions that allow satisfaction of these basic needs is thus a key predictor of whether or not people will display vitality and mental health" (pp. 229–230). To the degree that employers are able to set up conditions that contribute to meeting these needs, they are likely to have employees with better psychological health and lower levels of stress and burnout.

Reader Reflections

1) Are autonomy, competence, and relatedness core needs of yours?
2) Do you feel that these are generally well met in your life?
3) How do you see each of these needs being met within your organization?

People may react differently when their physiological needs are not met than when their psychological needs go unmet. When people do not have their physiological needs met, they will generally try harder and harder to get what they need. When people are hungry and do not get food right away, they will likely keep trying to find new ways to satisfy their hunger. Over time, they will likely do just about anything to get food. This is not always the case with psychological needs. People who have been deprived of love may continue to search for it, or they may close themselves off from it. Similarly, if people at work are thwarted in their efforts to achieve autonomy, competence, and relatedness, they might keep striving to meet these needs, or they might give up. When workers give up on meeting these needs they may become less autonomous and less inclined to strive for competence and connection with others. This may, in turn, hamper their ability to work effectively with coworkers and colleagues. It thus seems to be in an organization's best interest to set up an environment that is conducive to assisting staff in meeting their needs and accomplishing their goals. Suggestions for creating conditions to help employees meet these are described in the following paragraphs.

The Psychologically Healthy Workplace Program suggests that efforts to create a psychologically healthier workplace can be divided into five categories: *employee involvement, work-life balance, employee growth and development, health and safety,* and *employee recognition* (Grawitch, Gottschalk, & Munz, 2006). Making changes in each of these categories can assist employees in meeting each of the psychological needs discussed in the preceding paragraphs.

Employee involvement. Much research over many years has documented that when people are involved in the decisions that affect them, they tend to have a more positive attitude, higher job satisfaction, lower turnover and burnout, and be more engaged and committed (Batt & Valcour, 2003; Grawitch, Trares, & Kohler, 2007). Research also suggests that employee involvement can result in a physically and psychologically healthier workplace (Grawitch, Ledford, Ballard, & Barber, 2009). The type of employee involvement that seems to be most effective in creating real change involves a bottom-up, rather than top-down, approach to understanding challenges and creating solutions. This type of approach to organizational development and change clearly fits with the social work value of client (worker) self-determination.

Grawitch and colleagues (2009) stated that effective employee involvement programs require a partnership between employees and employers. They recommend that employees be involved in the entire process of determining organizational and employee health needs and establishing healthy workplace practices, programs, and policies. Examples of approaches to employee involvement include the following:

- Conducting employee opinion surveys to determine where challenges around health and safety exist in the organization. These can be done initially to begin the process of creating organizational change and also periodically to evaluate how effective new programs are and to identify new types of need.
- Having regular employee forums to discuss issues that arise in the workplace and provide feedback and suggestions for alternative approaches.
- Creating employee teams to assess and develop programs to address a need that is identified.
- Developing a participative decision-making structure where employees have a say or a vote in decisions that affect their work.
- Creating self-managed work teams in which employees in the team have the primary responsibility for determining the best way to meet the goals that the organization has for the team.

Employee involvement can also include efforts to engage staff in activities that increase a sense of relatedness, both to others at work and to the organization in general. Creating rituals, as described in *Rituals of Resiliency,* can

Rituals of Resiliency

Author and organizational consultant, Bruce Anderson* (Community Activators, 2005), encourages agencies to develop rituals that are aimed at building a resilient workforce. Rituals can be understood as acts that are regularly repeated in a particular manner. They are said to be at the core of any well-functioning community. Organizational rituals devoted to the self-care of employees might include the following:

- Sharing a meal that reflects varying cultural groups at a monthly staff meeting
- Participating in a planned time in which workers can walk, laugh, or stretch
- Engaging in activities focused on discovering and using employee talents
- Celebrating holidays, birthdays, and new/retiring workers
- Recognizing employee successes and accomplishments

  What kinds of rituals would work well in your organization?
  What support would you need to begin implementing rituals of resiliency?

*For more information, visit Bruce Anderson's Web site at http://www.community activators.com.

assist in this process, while supporting the self-care of workers in creative and innovative ways.

Reader Reflections

1) In what ways are employees involved in analyzing issues and decision making in your agency?
2) Do you feel that your voice matters at your organization?
3) Do you feel that you are generally included in the decisions at work that affect you and your job?

To have real employee involvement requires a supportive climate in the workplace, which has been found by researchers to be an important component to meeting all three types of needs described in the self-determination theory (Lynch, Plant, & Ryan, 2005; Van den Broeck, Vansteenkiste, De Witte, & Lens, 2008). A supportive climate means a variety of things. First, it means that there must be a commitment from management not only to solicit employee input, but also to actually use the input. The desire for involvement must be genuine, as employees know quickly when they are asked for input that no one at the top wants to hear or plans to use. An insincere or cursory approach to line staff involvement merely serves to increase frustration and stress.

Another important component of a supportive climate is a sense of inter-personal safety. Employees cannot truly be involved, genuine, and share what is really on their minds if they do not feel safe. *Interpersonal safety* refers to people knowing that they will not be chastised, punished, or ridiculed for speaking up, even when what they have to say might challenge conventional wisdom within the organization. Having the freedom to speak up helps meet two of the needs described in self-determination theory. It encourages autonomy by allowing employees more control over their work and the workplace environment. It also helps develop better relationships between coworkers by encouraging people to be their authentic selves and say what is really on their minds.

Interpersonal safety and speaking up might also mean that staff members feel safe enough to ask for help when they are struggling. Having the opportunity to ask questions, get assistance, and process difficult situations and emotions is encouraged and even required in some organizations and discouraged and possibly punished in others. One can argue that the need for help, support, and time to process challenging experiences is particularly strong in social work environments. Yet staff may not feel safe enough to do so in some settings. An example of this can be seen in the following statement made by a participant in one of our focus groups:

> One of the things that I have seen that has traumatized workers—I don't think I'm exaggerating this—is the disconnect between administration and line staff. Decisions are made that impact line staff when administrators don't have any grasp of how that's going to affect the work that we're doing. For instance, we had to cut a lot of groups and individual counseling because of budget cuts. But we were told not to tell the clients that it was because of budget cuts. So we thought, "What are we supposed to tell them? That we don't like them any more?" They have a right to know why programs are being cut so they can advocate. If I had to put a visual on it, I'd think of being shackled. Your hands and feet are tied, you have no freedom, but you're supposed to do the same amount of work. It resulted in a lot of illnesses, a lot of union

grievances, a lot of medical stress. The worst part is that people are afraid to speak up; I think that's one of the biggest things. People are afraid of being retaliated against. I feel fortunate that I'm 60 years old because I'm not afraid any more. I have coworkers that are just coming to work for the county, just starting to get their feet on the ground financially, and they are scared to death to say anything. They come to me and tell me things that happened and they can't say anything for fear of losing their jobs. Part of the trauma for me is that I have to sit with those secrets. I get really frustrated with that. I cannot in good conscience encourage them to jeopardize their jobs. I've been here for 15 years; I know what happens to them. I see how they're destroyed in the system. It's scary, very scary.

Reader Reflections

1) Do you feel a sense of interpersonal safety at work? What would it take for you to feel truly interpersonally safe there?
2) What policies and practices have you seen in any work environment that encourage interpersonal safety?
3) What policies and practices would you like to see implemented in your workplace that would increase the likelihood of interpersonal safety?

Work–Life balance. Research conducted over several decades has noted the challenge for workers in finding a balance between work demands and home, family, and leisure activities. MacDermid (2005) found that more than 180 articles had been published about the conflict between balancing work and family lives. More than 30 years ago, Kanter (1977) noted that it is a myth to believe that work and home life can be truly separated from each other. What is happening at work often invades our home lives, and what is happening at home is brought to work. In addition, the U.S. value that supports long hours at work and little vacation time makes finding time to complete all of our work and home demands extremely difficult. New technologies, such as smart phones, have increased the challenge of keeping job-related issues at work and keeping family matters at home. It is easier to keep connected with family while at work and to receive e-mails and other work communications while at home. This can have an effect on both focus and productivity at work and work-free time at home. It can also further complicate efforts to set boundaries between work and home life and achieve work–life balance.

There are, however, measures that organizations can take to assist workers in developing balance that leads to better self-care. These include the following:

Flexible work schedules: Flexible work schedules are not new, and research suggests that employees find them helpful in balancing home and work lives and reducing stress (Hayman, 2009). Most flextime programs allow employees to have some flexibility in setting their hours, on the basis of some parameters. For example, a policy may state that employees must work 40 hours per week and be at work Monday through Thursday from 10:00 to 2:00. Other than those hours, they can schedule the remaining hours as best fits their lives and other obligations. To find flextime programs that really work for social workers, it is suggested that administrators solicit input from employees as to their needs. They should make clear, however, that individual worker needs must be balanced with the needs of clients and the organization. An expansion on the idea of flexible schedules has come to be known as a *results only work environment* (Ressler & Thompson, 2008). This approach to scheduling focuses more on outcomes than on hours worked. It means that employees know what they need to accomplish, and must get it done. But they can do it in the hours and in locations that work best for them.

Telecommuting options: In many jobs there is work that employees do that does not need to be completed at the office or in the field. There are times when employees can work from home or another location, thus reducing commute time and increasing time with family. Employers can work jointly with employees to determine how much of their assigned time could realistically be done from home and build that into their weekly or monthly schedules.

Family leave policies: An important component of work–life balance is the ability to take time off from work to meet family needs. Most industrialized countries offer paid maternity leave, and many countries offer paid parental leave, allowing both mothers and father to have paid time off after children are born. In the United States, the Family and Medical Leave Act of 1993 (P.L. 103-3) requires that employers in larger companies give employees 12 weeks of job-protected, unpaid leave for medical issues and family needs. This puts many new parents in a challenging situation if they cannot afford time off without pay. Twelve weeks is also a short period of time to spend with a new born before going back to work. Employers can support work–life balance by allowing employees to take more time off without the threat of losing their jobs. This can be supported by flexible work schedules and offsite work options that were described previously.

From the Field: Flextime

As a social worker with a large full-time caseload in a job that can be very emotionally draining, my self-care must be top priority. Arriving home to a handful of kids and a husband with their own needs and schedules, though enjoyable, does not always fulfill my self-care needs. I have learned that creating a balance between work, family, self, and all the other things that come with life is important. Working eight to five, Monday through Friday with the occasional overtime hours, does not allow for incorporating everything that has to be done in a busy schedule. Usually there is not much room for self-care on the weekends, and most mothers like me put it aside for another day.

The agency I work for used to allow a flexible or alternative schedule. This was a wonderful thing for my family and me. At the time I worked nine hours a day Monday through Thursday. That allowed me to take every other Friday off. My team and I alternated Fridays, and others alternated Mondays so there was always coverage. This worked out well for us personally, and we were more productive as a team. Having the extra day off in the week to do whatever needed to be done was a huge stress reliever. This was a great time to run errands and take care of doctor's appointments when the businesses were open, instead of taking extra time off work to do so. I could also take care of myself without feeling guilty that my family was being neglected. On most Fridays the kids were in school and my husband was at work; my schedule was the only thing on the agenda. It was a wonderful thing.

For some reason my agency took away the alternate work schedule, and I have personally had a harder time finding balance to take care of all the important things. Also, I have noticed morale has not been what it used to be. In fact, I have avoided the break room since this change because it seems that is where people congregate to vent. Adding graduate school to this equation has been especially difficult. I have used all my accrued sick time and most of my vacation time just to make sure I stay caught up with the necessities. Looking back, when we had the alternative schedule I was able to be more productive at work and at home in a way that was less stressful and more balanced.

—*Michelle*

Assistance with Child or Elder Care: Because of the rising numbers of single parents in the workforce and dual-wage earning families, it is increasingly important for organizations to consider approaches to helping employees attend to family needs. One such approach involves assisting workers in providing child care and care that is needed for other relatives. Flextime, telecommuting, and family leave policies can help with this. Providing on-site child care or partnering with other agencies to develop child care programs can also be of assistance. Organizations can also be flexible in allowing employees to come in a bit late or leave a bit early to pick up or drop off their children at school or daycare.

Vacation policies: As is the case with family leave policies, jobs in the United States come with far less vacation time than do jobs in other industrialized countries. The Center for Economic and Policy Research dubbed the United States the "no vacation nation," noting that we are the only advanced economy in which the government does not guarantee workers any paid holidays or vacations (Ray & Schmitt, 2007). Employers can help employees take better care of themselves and their families by creating a real vacation policy, paid if at all possible, under which employees are encouraged to stay off e-mail and ignore phone messages from work. Employers can further support real time off by not e-mailing or calling people about work matters when they are taking time off. This suggestion was raised by a number of the participants in our focus groups.

Employee growth and development: A common barrier to meeting employees' needs for competence and autonomy is inadequate opportunities for them to acquire new knowledge and skills so that they can increase their level of expertise. If a person does not have the skills or knowledge necessary to work effectively, he or she will likely not feel competent in the work or want to direct the work and complete it on his or her own. This is particularly true of new employees or interns who are still learning to do the job. In addition, environments in which employees do not have opportunities for learning are often ones that have few opportunities for advancement. If they do advance, workers may not feel, or actually be, competent for higher level work. Thus, a psychologically healthy organization with a supportive climate assists staff in obtaining job-related skills and knowledge so that they feel competent in their work, can work autonomously, and have the skills and knowledge necessary for advancement.

Employee growth and development can be furthered through ongoing in-house or outside training seminars. Smaller agencies can join forces with other agencies to share the cost of training for staff. In addition, coaching, mentoring, and leadership programs can support employee growth, as can tuition support or a flexible work schedule to assist them in obtaining an advanced degree. As staff members gain skill and knowledge, it is important for management to support their use of these skills without unnecessary micromanaging from above. Spreitzer and Porath (2012) also noted that support for employee growth and development means ensuring that staff have discretion in decision making. Employees are less stressed and afraid if they know that they can make decisions that affect their work and that they will be supported in the decisions that they do make. They add that employees can make good decisions when they have a broad range of information about the organization. This requires that information is openly and honestly shared at all levels of the agency.

Health and safety: Developing and maintaining health and safety initiatives can support the creation of physically and psychologically healthy workplaces. It is obviously important that employees understand the risks of their jobs and know about how to keep themselves safe in potentially dangerous situations. The level of risk for injury can be related to issues of interpersonal safety discussed previously. If employees do not feel safe asking questions or expressing their fears, they may not tell supervisors about unsafe situations and their perceived inability to handle them. Ongoing safety trainings are also important in helping social workers prepare for dangerous situations. Another approach to promoting the health and safety of employees entails the use of policies and practices that support the maintenance of healthy lifestyles. For example, employers might offer programs related to various self-care practices, including smoking cessation, nutrition, mindfulness activities, and exercise. Agencies could also suggest or offer activity classes at lunch or before or after work. Managers or supervisors might also encourage staff members to join together to commit to some type of self-care activity. A designated space can be provided for brief periods of rejuvenation, as is described in *Create Your Rejuvenation Room*. Time can be devoted to talking about what is working and what would make these efforts more successful. In addition, employers can offer onsite health screenings or let staff know when and where screenings are available in the community. Time off to partake in a screening would ideally be given.

Employee recognition: Employers can develop policies, programs, and practices that recognize individual employees and employee teams. The latter can encourage effective cooperation and collaboration. All types of employee recognition can make employees feel valued, appreciated, and acknowledged for the hard work that they are doing. This process can improve morale and encourage employee autonomy and feelings of competence. There are many approaches to employee recognition. Agencies can develop awards and conduct ceremonies recognizing the attainment of certain goals or for outstanding work. They can highlight some type of individual or group achievement in a monthly newsletter, in an e-mail, or via an announcement at a staff meeting.

Create Your Rejuvenation Room

The self-care and health of employees can be furthered when they have access to space designed to promote self-care and rejuvenation. Within a big enough office, a small room might be designated for this purpose. It might be decorated with calming pictures, plants, and a small water fountain. A specific location within the room might even be designed for stretching or meditation. When stressed, workers might have the option to go the Rejuvenation Room, sit in silence, and practice deep breathing or another mindfulness activity, as described in chapter 4.

If space is at a premium at your organization, consider the creation of a smaller Silent Space. This might be a cubical with a "Do Not Disturb" sign posted outside. Inside the cubical, a worker might find a soothing photograph displayed on the screen saver of a computer and a white noise machine for use in drowning out nearby conversations. Or perhaps they would have access to earphones that are set to play relaxing music. Brief respite periods in the Rejuvenation Room or Silent Space might do wonders with regard to improving the overall functioning and productivity of staff members.

- Take a few moments to conceive of a design for an interior of a Rejuvenation Room or Silent Space for your agency.
- Consider how you would "make the case" for the devotion of agency resources in this way.

Small gifts can be given as recognition of work well done. In addition, supervisors can be trained to note and acknowledge good work by their supervisees.

Reader Reflections

1) What policies do you see in your workplace that encourage employee involvement, work–life balance, employee growth and development, health and safety, and employee recognition?
2) Have any of these policies helped you to reduce stress or increase self-care?

Incorporating Inclusion

In addition to creating a psychologically safe work place, stress can be reduced in agencies by creating an inclusive workplace. Chapter 6 addresses issues of diversity in the workplace, noting that diversity is the mix of people from different upbringings, cultures, racial–ethnic groups, genders, abilities, ages, religions, learning styles, sexual orientations, gender identities, and classes. Over the years, most organizations have come to understand the importance of recruiting a diverse workforce and avoiding discrimination. However, taking the next step, and becoming an inclusive organization has often proven more difficult. As Kettleborough (2005) noted,

> However worthy and admirable the notion, the actual task of bridging the gap between token 'diversity' and real 'inclusion' remains monumental. We have to unravel generations of bigotry, prejudice and ignorance and sometimes dismantle entire social, organizational and community structures, to travel each step on this road. (p. 8)

Whereas social workers may be more apt to understand the need for inclusion, we are not necessarily more likely to practice it than are people in other fields. One example of this can be seen in the *NASW Standards for Cultural Competence in Social Work Practice* (NASW, 2001). Standard 7 notes that social workers should support and advocate for policies and practices that ensure a diverse workforce. This is essential for the work that we do. What is missing from this standard, however, is a focus on the need for social workers to support the inclusion of diverse workers across all levels of organizational activity.

It is easy to understand why a diverse, but not inclusive, workplace can be stressful. In these organizations, people who are outside of the mainstream for any reason are not fully accepted for who they are. When employees from diverse backgrounds do not feel included in the workplace, it may affect their satisfaction level, the services they provide, and their physical and mental health (McNeely, 1992). One way to understand why noninclusive environments produce stress is to consider the dual perspective framework, which was briefly discussed in chapter 1. This framework situates people as a part of two systems: the larger, dominant society system and the smaller system comprising their immediate environment (Anderson, Hayashi, & Frost, 2009). The latter can include family and the various communities to which many people belong. People who differ from dominant culture in any way develop two self-images and must move back and forth between two worlds—leaving a part of themselves at home and adhering to dominant culture—which can produce stress. This can influence how people dress, what they eat, what music they listen to, whether they acknowledge valued holidays and rituals, and how much of their lives they share with others. When people do bring their second self-image and set of behaviors into a noninclusive workplace, they can be judged, excluded, or ridiculed. This can add tremendous stress to a person's work life.

Reader Reflections

1) Which of your social identities or personal characteristics do you feel are included and welcomed at your organization? Are there parts of you that you feel you must keep hidden at work?

2) Do you notice gaps in inclusion at your organization? Are some groups of people less welcomed, listened to, and included than others?

3) Can you see ways in which a lack of inclusion adds stress to your workplace, either for you or for your coworkers or clients?

There are a number of approaches that organizations can take to achieve inclusion of diverse staff members. These efforts are generally consistent with one of two broad models (Gallop & Este, 2007). The first is a consensus-oriented model known as managing diversity (MD), wherein the focus is usually on developing an organization in which staff members are culturally competent and there are genuine recruitment efforts focused on bringing in diverse clients and staff. An underlying assumption of this model is that the basic structure of the organization is sound and the change that needs to occur is in employee beliefs and attitudes, and possibly some small organizational assumptions. The model stresses that people can reach consensus and work together and that conflict is not necessary or particularly helpful. The second model, multicultural organizational development (MCOD), is a conflict-oriented model. It assumes that for real inclusion to occur, major structural changes will likely need to be made within the organization. This can include a shift in the power dynamics. Given that, the model assumes that conflict and struggle will be necessary and beneficial. Change efforts within both models can begin with administrators speaking with employees to determine what the current climate feels like to them, what their needs are in terms of inclusion, and what they would suggest for improvements. This bottom-up approach supports employee involvement and buy in and makes it more likely that the solution will actually fit the problem.

The MD model assumes that achieving a diverse workforce and client base is important, but that it is not enough. For diversity to become inclusion involves active management. MD has more of a micro focus on policies and practices that are aimed at changing individual employees so that they are more inclusive of others. Often, a MD approach promotes the use of diversity trainings for staff, ideally focusing on the broad range of differing values and identities that exist in the organization. Training sessions can include conversations about truly valuing diversity and its benefits for employees, clients, and the organization. They often cover legal mandates and processes in which people can engage to reduce prejudice and discrimination. The MD model also focuses on improving access for diverse client groups and shaping interventions to more effectively meet client needs. This approach to inclusion is often structured in such a way as to minimize conflict (Gallop & Este, 2007). This can mean that real conflicts that exist are ignored and thus are not resolved. Some have argued that it is important to allow space for conflict in the diversity training process. They note that well managed conflict can bring about real change. It is important for administrators and supervisors who are developing or importing diversity trainings to examine their feelings about conflict and whether allowing or even encouraging it ultimately benefits the organization.

Some authors have argued that, although important, an individual focus on change in not adequate. To achieve a truly inclusive workplace, there is a need to examine and possibly change the power structure and leadership that exist in organizations. The MCOD model has more of a macro focus on creating structural change within organizations so that all components welcome diverse people and viewpoints. This requires sincere commitment from senior management to become receptive to the possibility of including diverse individuals within the top levels of administration. The philosophy behind MCOD differs from models such as MD, in that it involves meaningful change in the organization so that all people are truly welcome. MCOD attacks institutional discrimination and oppression rather than individual bias and behavior.

The MCOD process begins by creating a change team in the organization that comprises major stakeholders, possibly including administrators, staff at various levels, clients, and community partners. The team works with an external consultant to engage in the change process. The second phase is the support building phase, in which team members and the consultant assess the current status of diversity and inclusion in the organization and begin to get staff on board for the effort. This often includes gathering staff and client perceptions and attitudes about diversity and inclusion. This phase can be difficult if a great deal of criticism is raised and staff or administrators become angry or defensive. Areas in which there does not appear to be support for diversity and inclusion can then be addressed. The third phase of the process, multicultural leadership development, involves building support among administrators and other organizational leaders, such as board members. This moves past lip service for diversity and inclusion to a real commitment to make needed changes. This part of the process can include the development of a vision and mission statement in which inclusion is central and a system that rewards staff for furthering diversity and inclusion efforts. In this model, administrators should ideally be role models in the practice of and commitment to an inclusive workplace. The fourth phase, known as the multicultural systems change, involves conducting an analysis of feedback on current structures and developing intervention, implementation, and evaluation plans to address areas in the organization that hinder true inclusion. The analysis can examine leadership structure and ways that diverse people can become leaders in the organization. It can also look at recruitment of staff and clients, the types of interventions used, and many facets of organizational culture, some of which were described in chapter 6. Where barriers to inclusion are found, change plans are developed and evaluated for success. Although this process is somewhat labor intensive (Hyde, 2004), it holds potential for creating increasingly healthy and productive organizations.

Valuing Vision

Agencies that act in accordance with their organizational vision operationalize their values in shaping their work with clients and communities and in guiding how they treat their employees. As noted in chapter 6, organizational vision statements are traditionally written to express an agency's broad view of the change they want to create in the external environment. Thus, valuing vision can mean ensuring that the organization is doing everything possible to improve conditions for clients and communities and is following their stated values in the work that they do. This is important for several reasons. Research has found that employees are more likely to thrive, rather than just survive at work, when they believe that the work they do is important (Spreitzer & Porath, 2012). Given the nature of social work, this is particularly important in our field. When the work that an organization is doing is not effectively moving staff toward their vision of improved lives for their client population, they may not feel that they are making a difference. In addition, when agencies behave in ways that go against their stated vision and values, this can cause a disconnect for employees and result in added stress. The following examples may help illustrate these points:

- An organization that works with the LGBTQ community has a vision of a healthier and safer community. They know that alcoholism rates are higher among individuals in the LGBTQ community than they are in the general population, that intimate partner violence goes up with increased alcohol use, and that alcohol use can increase the risk of unsafe sexual activity. The organization expresses values of health, safety, and nonviolence. Yet, when fundraising becomes a challenge in a bad economy, they accept money from an alcohol producer.
- An agency states that they value client self-determination and the use of best practices in serving their target population. Yet they provide only one model of service that does not meet the needs of some clients. The practice model they use was determined by funders who only allow one approach to service delivery.

These two vision challenges came about because organizations need funding. Acquiring adequate funding is a particular challenge during the economic downturn the United States has experienced since 2007. Thus, organizations may take money where they can get it. Additional challenges with vision occur as a result of restrictions placed on social work agencies by state laws, as can be seen in the following example:

A state passes a law that prohibits providing any information about sex in public schools. This limits the work that can be done by groups focused on preventing the spread of HIV among youth. Let us assume that research shows that prevention efforts that do not include information about safe sexual practices are ineffective. Employees must then engage in their work knowing that it does not match the agency values of meeting client needs and incorporating best practices and that it does not meet the agency vision of creating a community in which youth are safe and healthy.

In previous examples, employees are working in environments in which they experience value clashes or engage in their work knowing that it is not as effective as it could be. Organizations can reduce employee stress by adhering to vision and values and by doing all they can to demonstrate both daily. However, organizations cannot avoid all conflict. In cases in which conflicts do arise, open and honest communication can help employees see why deviation from the vision or values might be needed. If employers are following some of the practices noted previously, such as including employees in the decision-making process, staff will have a say in deciding whether deviations are necessary. At the very least they will understand why difficult decisions must be made and how they are in the best long-term interests of the organization.

The second component to valuing vision involves acting toward employees in a way that is consistent with the organization's treatment of clients and community. Consider the agency that speaks about justice in their vision statement yet treats employees unjustly. Or imagine one that advocates for healthier, lower stress lives for clients yet does little to promote the health and self-care of employees. Many of us have seen situations in our field in which agencies advocate for healthy family policies for those in the community yet expect employees to sacrifice family time to work overtime. This incongruence can be quite stressful for employees and can result in the belief that they are unsupported or disrespected by their organization. Social work agencies that are serious about reducing stress and supporting self-care must take a good look at their employment policies and practices. This process can begin with a concerted effort to better understand the ways in which the organization's vision can be accessed to support workplace wellness.

Conclusion

Some people might be concerned that if an organization is focusing on stress reduction, inclusion, and self-care for employees that there will be less of a focus on clients and productivity. However, research suggests that this is not the case. Workers who have lower levels of stress and are generally happier on the job are also more productive and more committed to the organization (Gilbert, 2012). Spitzer and Porath (2012) noted that it is important that organizations care about the well-being of their staff members:

> In our research into what makes for a consistently high-performing workforce, we've found good reason to care: happy employees produce more than unhappy ones over the long term. They routinely show up for work, they're less likely to quit, they go above and beyond the call of duty, and they attract people who are just as committed to the job. Moreover, they're not sprinters, they're more like marathon runners, in it for the long haul. (p. 93)

Thus, efforts toward creating healthy work environments for employees promote the productivity, effectiveness, and stability of social service organizations. They also contribute to the creation of a high-functioning workforce that is needed to ensure a strong future for the profession of social work.

Questions for Discussion

1. Discuss the three core needs (autonomy, competence, and relatedness) that Deci and Ryan (2000) noted in the self-determination theory. Are they actually core needs of yours? Are you meeting these three needs in your work or internship? If so, how are they being met? If not, what do you think is keeping you from effectively meeting them?

2. What does a supportive workplace climate mean to you? Is the climate at your organization supportive, either on the basis of your definition or on those given in the chapter? If so, what makes it supportive? If not, what would make it more supportive?

3. Discuss whether it is an employer's responsibility to help employees find work–life balance or if it is the employee's responsibility to make this happen. Why do you think so? Why might some employers want to help employees have better work–life balance?

4. Discuss the difference between diversity and inclusion. Which do you see more of at your organization? What do you see as barriers to diversity at the organization? What do you see as barriers to inclusion at the organization?

5. Discuss the importance of having an organizational vision statement. Does your organization have a written vision statement? If not, do you know what the vision of the organization is? In what ways do you see the agency valuing vision? In what ways do you see its vision being ignored?

Chapter Exercises

1. Self-Care Policies

Try to determine whether your agency has any written policies that are aimed at reducing employee stress or encouraging self-care. If so, why were the policies instituted? Are they being implemented? Do you believe that they are successful?

2. Policy for Psychological Safety

Write a new workplace policy that you believe would make your organization more psychologically healthy. Would the new policy meet any of the three needs noted in Deci and Ryan's (2000) self-determination theory? How would it fit into any of the categories that researchers have suggested make up psychologically safe workplaces (employee involvement, work–life balance, employee growth and development, health and safety and employee recognition)?

3. Inclusivity

Spend some time looking at your organization to determine how inclusive it seems to be for people of different genders, races–ethnicities, sexual orientations, gender identities, abilities, ages, political ideologies, socioeconomic statuses, and religions. What indicators do you see that people from a range of backgrounds and identities are welcomed and supported? What indicators do you see to suggest that some groups of people are less included than others?

Final Thoughts

We would like to end this book on a note of hope. This is not difficult, because signs of hope abound in our profession as it relates to taking on the challenges that we have discussed. Students of social work are now increasingly interested in learning about work-related stress and self-care. Workers in the field are willing to share their stories of trauma, distress, and burnout to help others. They are also intensely interested in processing stressful experiences and exchanging ideas for coping with the mutual challenges that they face. Many are prepared to assist their colleagues in reframing traumatizing events, in finding needed collegial or supervisory support, and in attaining a state of balance between work and home life responsibilities. Most enjoy sharing a hearty laugh about the unexpected and unusual events that are part and parcel of the work we do. Although stress is clearly a threat to the functioning of social workers, a counterforce prevails. It is the force that propels us to come together to uncover undesirable circumstances and create needed change. It is also the impetus toward solution building that leverages our own and others' strengths and capabilities. Finally, it is the momentum that makes possible the continued evolution of the field of social work.

References

Acker, G. M. (2003). Role conflict and ambiguity: Do they predict burnout among mental health service providers? *Journal of Social Work in Mental Health, 1*, 63–80.

Alkema, K., Linton, J., & Davies, R. (2008). A study of the relationship between self-care, compassion satisfaction, compassion fatigue, and burnout among hospice professionals. *Journal of Social Work in End-of-Life & Palliative Care, 4*, 101–119.

American Psychological Association. (2011, March 8). *APA survey finds many U.S. workers feel stressed out and undervalued* [Press release]. Retrieved from http://www.apa.org/news/press/releases/2011/03/workers-stressed.aspx

Anderson, W., Hayashi, R., & Frost, C. J. (2009). Measuring diversity awareness of social work students: The dual perspective inventory. *Journal of Teaching in Social Work, 29*, 258–270.

Anschuetz, B. (1999). The high cost of caring: Coping with workplace stress. *Ontario Association of Children's Aid Societies Journal, 43*(2), 17–21.

Argyris, M., & Schon, D. (1974). *Theory in practice.* San Francisco: Jossey-Bass.

Aspinwall, L. G., & Taylor, S. E. (1997). A stitch in time: Self-regulation and proactive coping. *Psychological Bulletin, 121*, 417–436.

Azar, S. T. (2000). Preventing burnout in professionals and paraprofessionals who work with child abuse and neglect cases: A cognitive behavioral approach to supervision. *JCLP: In Session: Psychotherapy in Practice, 56*, 643–663.

Bandura, A. (1995). *Self-efficacy in changing societies.* New York: Cambridge University Press.

Bandura, A. (1997). *Self-efficacy: The exercise of control.* New York: W. H. Freeman.

Barnes, I. (2006). Coping with workplace stress. *Canadian Nursing Home, 17*, 19–24.

Barofsky, I. (1978). Compliance, adherence and the therapeutic alliance: Steps in the development of self-care. *Social Science and Medicine, 12*, 369–376.

Batt, R., & Valcour, M. (2003). Human resource practices as predictors of work–family outcomes and employee turnover. *Industrial Relations: A Journal of Economy and Society, 42*, 189–220.

Beck, A. T., Rush, J. A., Shaw. B. F., & Emery, G. (1979). *Cognitive therapy of depression.* New York: Guilford Press.

Bell, J. L. (1995). Traumatic event debriefing: Service delivery designs and the role of social work. *Social Work, 40,* 36–43.

Berg, I. K., & Kelly, S. (2000). *Building solutions in child protective services.* New York: W. W. Norton.

Bernotavicz, F. (1997). *Retention of child welfare caseworkers: A report.* Retrieved from http://muskie.usm.maine.edu/helpkids/pubstext/retention.html

Billings, A. G., & Moos, R. H. (1981). The role of coping responses and social resources in attenuating the stress of life events. *Journal of Behavioral Medicine, 4,* 139–157.

Bishop, S. R., Lau, M., Shapiro, S., Carlson, L., Anderson, N. D., Carmody, J., et al. (2004). Mindfulness: A proposed operational definition. *Clinical Psychology: Science and Practice, 11,* 230–241.

Bolte Taylor, J. (2006). *My stroke of insight: A brain scientist's personal journey.* New York: Viking.

Bond, S. A., Tuckey, J. R., & Dollard, M. F. (2010). Psychosocial safety climate, workplace bullying, and symptoms of posttraumatic stress. *Organizational Development Journal, 28,* 37–56.

Boudrias, J., Desrumauz, P., Gaudreau, P., Nelson, K., Brunet, L., & Savoie, A. (2011). Modeling the experience of psychological health at work: The role of personal resources, social-organizational resources, and job demands. *International Journal of Stress Management, 18,* 372–395.

Bourn, D., & Bootle, K. (2005). Evaluation of a distance learning, post graduate advanced award in social work programme for child and family social work supervisors and mentors. *Social Work Education, 24,* 343–362.

Brenner, C. (1985). Countertransference as compromise formation. *Psychoanalytic Quarterly, 68,* 379–406.

Briar, S. (1974). The future of social work: An introduction. *Social Work, 19,* 514–518.

Bride, B. (2007). Prevalence of secondary traumatic stress among social workers. *Social Work, 52,* 63–70.

Brown, B. (2010). *The gifts of imperfection: Let go of who you think you're supposed to be and embrace who you are.* Center City, MN: Hazelden.

Brown, K. W., & Ryan, R. M. (2003). The benefits of being present: Mindfulness and its role in psychological well-being. *Journal of Personality and Social Psychology, 84,* 822–848.

Buie, D. H. (1981). Empathy: Misconceptions and misuses in psychotherapy. *American Journal of Psychiatry, 145,* 420–424.

Cannon, W. B. (1932). *The wisdom of the body.* New York: Peter Smith.

Carmody, J., Baer, R. A., Lykins, E.L.B., & Olendzki, N. (2009). An empirical study of the mechanisms of mindfulness in a mindfulness-based stress reduction program. *Journal of Clinical Psychology, 65,* 613–626.

Carver, C. S., Scheier, M. F., & Weintraub, J. K. (1989). Assessing coping strategies: A theoretically based approach. *Journal of Personality and Social Psychology, 56,* 267–283.

Caselman, T. D., & Brandt, M. D. (2007). School social workers' intent to stay. *School Social Work Journal, 31,* 33–48.

Catherall, D. R. (1999). Coping with secondary traumatic stress: The importance of the therapist's professional peer group. In H. Stamm (Ed.), *Secondary traumatic stress: Self-care issues for clinicians, researchers and educators.* Baltimore: Sidran Press.

CBS News. (2010). *The body's little-known signs of stress.* Retrieved from http://www.cbsnews.com/stories/2009/04/01/earlyshow/health/main4908820.shtml

Chamberlain, J., Watts, S., Mohide, P., Muggah, H., Trim, K., & Bantebya Kyomuhundo, G. (2007). Women's perception of self-worth and access to healthcare. *International Journal of Gynecology Obstetrics, 98,* 75–79.

Chödrön, P. (2002). *When things fall apart.* Boston: Shambhala.

Chopra, D. (1994). *The seven spiritual laws of success.* San Rafael, CA: Amber-Allen.

Chopra, D., Simon, D., & Backer, L. (2002). *The Chopra Center cookbook: Nourishing body and soul.* Hoboken, NJ: John Wiley & Sons.

Cocchiara, F. K., & Bell, M. P. (2009). Gender and work stress: Unique stressors, unique responses. In C. L. Cooper, J. C. Quick, & M. J. Schabracq (Eds.), *International handbook of work and health psychology* (pp. 123–145). Hoboken, NJ: Wiley-Blackwell.

Cohany, S. R., & Sok, E. (2007, February). Married mothers in the labor force: Trends in labor force participation of married mothers of infants. *Monthly Labor Review,* 9–16.

Cohen, B. Z. (1999). Intervention and supervision in strengths-based social work practice. *Families in Society: The Journal of Contemporary Human Services, 80,* 460–466.

Collins, M. (2006). Taking a lead on stress: Rank and relationship awareness in the NHS. *Journal of Nursing Management, 14,* 310–317.

Collins-Camargo, C., & Millar, K. (2010). The potential for a more clinical approach to child welfare supervision to promote practice and case outcomes: A qualitative study in four states. *Clinical Supervisor, 29,* 164–187.

Community Activators. (2005). *Rituals of resiliency.* Retrieved from http://www.placercollaborativenetwork.org/pastminutes/FallRetreat/HopePacketNov07.pdf

Cousins, C. (2004). Becoming a social work supervisor: A significant role transition. *Australian Social Work, 57,* 175–185.

Cox, K., & Steiner, S. (in press). Preserving commitment to social work service through the prevention of vicarious trauma. *Journal of Social Work Ethics and Values.*

Culture. (2012). *Merriam-Webster's Dictionary* [Online edition]. Retrieved from http://www.merriam-webster.com/dictionary/culture

Deci, E. L., & Ryan, R. M. (2000). The "what" and "why" of goal pursuits: Human needs and the self-determination behavior. *Psychological Inquiry, 11,* 227–268.

DePoy, E., & French Gilson, S. (2003). *Evaluation practice: Thinking and action principles for social work practice*. Pacific Grove, CA: Brooks/Cole.

Devilly, G. J., Wright, R., & Varker, T. (2009). Vicarious trauma, secondary traumatic stress, or simply burnout? Effect of trauma therapy on mental health professionals. *Australian and New Zealand Journal of Psychiatry, 43*, 373–385.

Dickinson, N. S., & Perry, R. E. (2002). Factors influencing the retention of specially educated public child welfare workers. *Journal of Health & Social Policy, 15*, 89–103.

Durkheim, E. (1964). *The division of labor in society*. New York: Free Press. (Original work published 1893)

Einarsen, S., Hoel, H., Zapf, D., & Cooper, C. L. (2003). The concept of bullying at work: The European tradition. In S. Einarsen, H. Hoel, D. Zapf, & C. L. Cooper (Eds.), *Bullying and emotional abuse in the workplace: International perspectives in research and practice* (pp. 145–162). London: Taylor & Francis.

Elavsky, S. (2010). Longitudinal examination of the exercise and self-esteem model in middle-aged women. *Journal of Sport & Exercise Psychology, 32*, 862–880.

Ellett, A. (2009). Intentions to remain employed in child welfare: The role of human caring, self-efficacy beliefs, and professional organizational culture. *Children and Youth Services Review, 31*, 78–88.

Ellis, A. (1984). How to deal with your most difficult client—you. *Psychotherapy in Private Practice, 2*, 25–35.

Elovainio, M., Kivimaki, M., & Helkama, K. (2001). Organizational justice evaluations, job control, and occupational strain. *Journal of Applied Psychology, 86*, 418–424.

Empathy. (2012). *Merriam-Webster's Dictionary* [Online edition]. Retrieved from http://www.merriam-webster.com/dictionary/empathy

Ertel, M. Stilijanow, U., Cvitkovic, J., & Lenhardt, U. (2008). Social policies, infrastructure and social dialogue in relation to psychosocial risk management. In S. Leka & T. Cox (Eds.), *The European Framework for Psychosocial Risk Management* (pp. 60–78). Nottingham, England: World Health Organization.

Family and Medical Leave Act of 1993, P.L. 103-3, 107 Stat. 6 (1993).

Figley, C. R. (1995). *Compassion fatigue: Coping with secondary traumatic stress disorder in those who treat the traumatized*. New York: Brunner-Routledge.

Fleming, L. M., Glass, J. A., Fujisaki, S., & Toner, S. L. (2010). Group process and learning: A grounded theory model of group supervision. *Training and Education in Professional Psychology, 4*, 194–203.

Folkman, S. (1997). Positive psychological states and coping with severe stress. *Social Science and Medicine, 45*, 1207–1221.

Folkman, S. (2008). The case for positive emotions in the stress process. *Anxiety, Stress, & Coping, 21*, 3–14.

Folkman, S., & Moskowitz, J. T. (2000). Stress, positive emotion, and coping. *Current Directions in Psychological Science, 9*, 115–118.

Folkman, S., & Moskowitz, J. T. (2004). Coping: Pitfalls and promise. *Annual Review of Psychology, 55*, 745–774.

Fowler, J. H., & Christakis, N. A. (2008). Dynamic spread of happiness in a large social network: Longitudinal analysis over 20 years in the Framingham Heart Study. *British Medical Journal, 337*, 1–9.

Freudenberger, H. J. (1974). Staff burnout. *Journal of Social Issues, 30*, 159–165.

Frost, P. J. (2007). *Toxic emotions at work and what you can do about them.* Boston: Harvard Business School Press.

Furlong, S. (1996). Self-care: The application of ward philosophy. *Journal of Clinical Nursing, 5*, 85–90.

Gallop, C. J., & Este, D. C. (2007). Multicultural organizational development (MCOD): The fundamental transformation of Canadian social work education. *International Journal of Diversity, 6*(4), 107–117.

Gantz, S. (1990). Self-care: Perspectives from six disciplines. *Holistic Nursing Practice, 4*, 1–12.

Garland, E., Gaylord, S., & Park, J. (2009). The role of mindfulness in positive reappraisal. *Journal of Science and Healing, 5*, 37–44.

Garnefski, N., Kraaij, V., & Spinhoven, P. (2001). Negative life events, cognitive emotion regulation, and emotional problems. *Personality and Individual Differences, 30*, 1311–1327.

Gentile, L., Ballou, M., Roffman, E., & Ritchie, J. (2010). Supervision for social change: A feminist ecological perspective. *Women & Therapy, 33*, 140–151.

Gentry, J. E. (2002). Compassion fatigue: A crucible of transformation. *Journal of Trauma Practice, 1*(3/4), 37–61.

Gilbert, D. (January/February 2012). The science behind the smile. *Harvard Business Review*, 85–90.

Glanz, K., Rimer, B. K., & Lewis, F. M. (2002). *Health behavior and health education: Theory, research and practice.* San Francisco: Wiley & Sons.

Godfrey, C. M., Harrison, M. B., Lysaght, R., Lamb, M., Graham, I. D., & Oakley, P. O. (2011). Care of self—care by other—care of other: The meaning of self-care from research, practice, policy, and industry perspectives. *International Journal of Evidence-Based Healthcare, 9*, 3–24.

Gold, N. (1998). Using participatory research to help promote the physical and mental health of female social workers in child welfare. *Child Welfare, 77*, 701–724.

Goleman, D. (1998, November–December). What makes a leader? *Harvard Business Review, 76*, 93–102.

Grandey, A. A. (2003). When the "show must go on." Surface acting and deep acting as determinants of emotional exhaustion and peer-rated service delivery. *Academy of Management Journal, 46*, 86–96.

Grawitch, M. J., Gottschalk, M., & Munz, D. C. (2006). The path to a healthy workplace: A critical review linking healthy workplace practices, employee well-being, and organizational improvements. *Consulting Psychology Journal: Practice and Research, 58*, 129–147.

Grawitch, M. J., Ledford, G. R., Ballard, D. W., & Barber, L. K. (2009). Leading the healthy workforce: The integral role of employee involvement. *Consulting Psychology Journal: Practice and Research, 61*(2), 122–135.

Grawitch, M. J., Trares, S. T., & Kohler, J. M. (2007). Healthy workplace practices and employee outcomes in a university context. *International Journal of Stress Management, 14,* 275–293.

Greenacre, P. (1971). *Emotional growth: Psychoanalytic studies of the gifted and a great variety of other individuals* (Vol. II). New York: International Universities Press.

Greenson, R. R. (1960). Empathy and its vicissitudes. *International Journal of Psychoanalysis, 41,* 418–424.

Hall, E. T. (1983). *The dance of life: The other dimension of time.* New York: Anchor Press/Doubleday.

Harkness, D. (1995). The art of helping in supervised practice: Skills, relationships and outcomes. *Clinical Supervisor, 13,* 63–76.

Harkness, D., & Hensley, H. (1991). Changing focus of social work supervision: Effects on client satisfaction and generalized contentment. *Social Work, 36,* 506–512.

Harvard Health Publications. (2010). *Stress management: Approaches for preventing and reducing stress.* Retrieved from http://www.health.harvard.edu/ special_health_reports/stress-management-approaches-for-preventing-and-reducing-stress

Harvard University. (2012). *Project Implicit.* Retrieved from http://www.project implicit.net

Haslam, S. A., O'Brien, A., Jetten, J., Vormedal, K., & Penna, S. (2005). Taking the strain: Social identity, social support and the experience of stress. *British Journal of Social Psychology, 44,* 355–370.

Haslam, S. A., & van Dick, R. (2011). A social identity approach to workplace stress. In D. De Cremer, R. van Dick, & J. K. Murnighan (Eds.), *Social psychology organizations* (pp. 325–352). New York: Routledge/Taylor & Francis.

Hayes, J. A. (1995). Countertransference in group psychotherapy: Waking a sleeping dog. *International Journal of Group Psychotherapy, 45,* 521–535.

Hayman, J. R. (2009). Flexible work arrangements: Exploring the linkages between perceived usability of flexible work schedules and work/life balance. *Community, Work & Family, 12,* 327–338.

Hays, K. F. (1999). Nutrition and exercise: Key components of taking care of yourself. In L. T. Pantano (Chair), *Taking care of yourself: The continuing quest.* Symposium conducted at the 107th Annual Conference of the American Psychological Association, Boston.

Head, J., Kivimaki, M., Siegrist, J., Ferrie, J. E., Vahterma, J., Shipley, M. J., et al. (2007). Effort–reward imbalance and relational injustice at work predict sickness absence: The Whitehall II study. *Journal of Psychosomatic Research, 63,* 433–440.

Henggeler, S. W., Melton, G. B., Brondino, M. J., Scherer, D. G., & Hanley, J. H. (1997). Multisystemic therapy with violent and chronic juvenile offenders and their families: The role of treatment fidelity in successful dissemination. *Journal of Consulting and Clinical Psychology, 65,* 821–833.

Henggeler, S. W., Schoenwald, S. K., Letourneau, J. G., & Edwards, D. L. (2002). Transporting efficacious treatments to field settings: The link between supervisory practices and therapist fidelity in MST programs. *Journal of Clinical Child and Adolescent Psychology, 31,* 155–167.

Hepworth, D. H., Rooney, R. H., Dewberry Rooney, G., Strom-Gottfried, K., & Larsen, J. (2010). *Direct social work practice: Theory and skills* (8th ed.). Belmont, CA: Brookes/Cole.

Hinkle, L. E. (1977). The concept of "stress" in the biological and social sciences. In Z. J. Lipowski, D. R. Lipsitt, & P. C. Shybrow (Eds.), *Psychosomatic medicine: Current trends and clinical implications* (pp. 27–49). New York: Oxford University Press.

Hofstede, G. H. (2001). *Culture's consequences: Comparing values, behaviors, institutions, and organizations across nations* (2nd ed.). Thousand Oaks, CA: Sage Publications.

House, R. J., Hanges, P. J., Javidan, M., Dorfman, P. W., & Gupin, V. (2004). *Culture, leadership, and organizations: The GLOBE study of 62 societies.* Thousand Oaks, CA: Sage Publications.

Hyde, C. (2004). Multicultural development in human services agencies: Challenges and solutions. *Social Work, 49,* 7–16.

Idris, M., Dollard, M. F., Coward, J., & Dorman, C. (2012). Psychosocial safety climate: Conceptual distinctiveness and effect on job demands and worker psychological health. *Safety Science, 50,* 19–28.

Jetten, J., Haslam, C., Haslam, S. A., & Branscombe, N. R. (2009). The social cure. *Scientific American Mind, 20,* 26–33.

Kadushin, A. (1985). *Supervision in social work* (2nd ed.). New York: Columbia University Press.

Kadushin, A., & Harkness. D. (2002*). Supervision in social work* (4th ed.). New York: Columbia University Press.

Kanter, R. M. (1977). *Work and family in the United States: A critical review and agenda for research and policy.* New York: Russell Sage Foundation.

Kearney, M., Weininger, R., Vachon, M., Harrison, R., & Mount, B. (2009). Self-care of physicians caring for patients at the end of life: "Being connected: A key to my survival." *Journal of the American Medical Association, 301,* 1155–1164.

Kettleborough, S. (2005). Investing in inclusion. *Management Services, 49,* 8–9.

Kickbusch, I. (1989). Self-care in health promotion. *Social Science and Medicine, 29,* 125–130.

Killian, K. D. (2008). Helping til it hurts? A multimethod study of compassion fatigue, burnout, and self-care in clinicians working with trauma survivors. *Traumatology, 14,* 32–44.

Kim, H., & Lee, S. Y. (2009). Supervisory communication: Burnout, and turnover intention among social workers in health care settings. *Social Work in Health Care, 48,* 364–385.

Kluckhohn, F. R., & Strodtbeck, F. L. (1961). *Variations in value orientation.* Westport, CT: Greenwood Press.

Knutson, K. L., Spiegel, K., Penev, P., & Van Cauter, E. (2007). The metabolic consequences of sleep deprivation. *Sleep Medicine Review, 11,* 163–178.

Kobasa, S. (1979). Stressful life events, personality, and health: An inquiry into hardiness. *Journal of Personality and Social Psychology, 37,* 1–11.

Kolb, D. A. (1984*). Experiential learning: Experience as the source of learning and development.* Englewood Cliffs, NJ: Prentice-Hall.

Korinek, A. W., & Kimball, T. G. (2003). Managing and resolving conflict in the supervisory system. *Contemporary Family Therapy, 25,* 295–310.

Kramer, R. M. (1999). Trust and distrust in organizations: Emerging perspectives, enduring questions. *Annual Review of Psychology, 50,* 569–598.

Kuper, H., Marmot, M., & Yamase, H. (2003). Job strain, job demands, decision latitude, and risk of coronary heart disease within the Whitehall II study. *Journal of Epidemiology and Community Health, 57,* 147–153.

Kuper, H., Sing-Manoux, A., Siegrist, J., & Marmot, M. (2002). When reciprocity fails: Effort–reward imbalance in relation to coronary heart disease and health functioning within the Whitehall II study. *Occupational Environmental Medicine, 59,* 777–784.

Lambert, V. A., Lambert, C. E., & Yamase, H. (2003). Psychological hardiness, workplace stress and related stress reduction strategies. *Nursing and Health Sciences, 5,* 181–184.

Landsman, M. J. (2001). Commitment in public child welfare. *Social Services Review, 75,* 386–419.

Lazarus, R. S. (1966). *Psychological stress and the coping process.* New York: McGraw-Hill.

Lazarus, R. S., & Cohen, J. B. (1977). Environmental stress. In I. Altman & J. F. Wohlwill (Eds.), *Human behavior and the environment: Current theory and research* (pp. 89–127). New York: Plenum Press.

Lazarus, R. S., & Folkman, S. (1984). Stress, appraisal, and coping. New York: Springer.

Letteney, S. (2010). Disrupted caregiving and maternal HIV disease: A proposed model for evaluating HIV affected children's psychological adjustment. *Social Work Health Care, 49,* 753–763.

Lietz, C. A., & Rounds, T. (2009). Strengths-based supervision: A child welfare supervision training project. *Clinical Supervisor, 28,* 124–140.

Linehan, M. (1993). *Skills training manual for treating borderline personality disorder.* New York: Guilford Press.

Linton, J. M., & Hedstrom, S. M. (2006). An exploratory qualitative investigation of group processes in group supervision: Perceptions of master's level practicum students. *Journal for Specialists in Group Work, 31,* 51–72.

Lynch, M. F., Plant, R. W., & Ryan, R. M. (2005). Psychological needs and threat to safety: Implications for staff and patients in a psychiatric hospital for youth. *Professional Psychology: Research and Practice, 36,* 415–425.

MacDermid, S. M. (2005). (Re)considering conflict between work and family. In E. E. Kossek & S. J. Lambert (Eds.), *Work and life integration: Organizational, cultural, and individual perspectives* (pp. 19–40). Mahwah, NJ: Lawrence Erlbaum.

Malawista, K. L. (2004). Rescue fantasies in child therapy: Countertransference/transference enactments. *Child and Adolescent Social Work Journal, 21,* 373–386.

Maslach, C. (2005). Understanding burnout: Work and family issues. In D. F. Halperin & S. E. Murphy (Eds.), *From work–family balance to work–family interaction: Changing the metaphor* (pp. 99–114). Mahwah, NJ: Lawrence Erlbaum.

Maslach, C., & Leiter, M. P. (2005a). Reversing burnout: How to rekindle your passion for your work. *Stanford Social Innovation Review, 1,* 43–449.

Maslach, C., & Leiter, M. P. (2005b). Stress and burnout: The critical research. In C. L. Cooper (Ed.), *Handbook of stress medicine and health* (2nd ed., pp. 153–170). Boca Raton, FL: CRC Press.

McCann, L., & Pearlman, L. A. (1990a). *Through a glass darkly: Understanding and treating the adult trauma survivor through constructivist self-development theory.* New York: Brunner/Mazel.

McCann, L., & Pearlman, L. A. (1990b). Vicarious traumatization: A framework for understanding the psychological effects of working with victims. *Journal of Traumatic Stress, 3,* 131–149.

McCormack, D. (2003). An examination of the self-care concept. *Nursing Leadership, 16,* 48–65.

McGeorge, C. R., & Carlson, T. S. (2010). Social justice mentoring: Preparing family therapists for social justice advocacy work. *Michigan Family Review, 14,* 42–59.

McGowan, J., Gardner, D., & Fletcher, R. (2006). Positive and negative affective outcomes of occupational stress. *New Zealand Journal of Psychology, 35,* 92–98.

McNeely, R. L. (1992). Job satisfaction in the public social services: Perspectives on structure, situational factors, gender, and ethnicity. In Y. Hasenfeld (Ed.), *Human services as complex organizations* (pp. 224–256). Newbury Park, CA: Sage Publications.

Meyer, I. H. (2003). Prejudice, social stress, and mental health in lesbian, gay, and bisexual populations: Conceptual issues and research evidence. *Psychological Bulletin, 129,* 674–697.

Milne, D., & Reiser, R. (2008, November). *Enhancing CBT supervision using evidence-based practices (EBS).* Paper presented at the ABCT Clinical Roundtable on Supervision, Orlando, FL.

Moos, R. H. (Ed.). (1977). *Coping with physical illness.* New York: Plenum Press.

Moran, C. C. (2002). Humor as a moderator of compassion fatigue. In C. R. Figley (Ed.), *Treating compassion fatigue* (pp. 139–154). New York: Brunner-Routledge.

Mor Barak, M. E., Nissly, J. A., & Levin, A. (2001). Antecedents to retention and turnover among child welfare, social work, and other human service employees: What can we learn from past research? A review and metanalysis. *Social Service Review, 75,* 625–637.

Mor Barak, M. E., Travis, D. J., Pyun, H., & Xie, B. (2009). The impact of supervision on worker outcomes: A meta-analysis. *Social Service Review, 83,* 3–32.

Morin, P. (2002). *Rank and salutogenesis: A quantitative and empirical study of self-rated health and perceived social status.* Unpublished doctoral dissertation, Union Institute and University, Cincinnati.

Morrison, T. (1990). The emotional effects of child protection work on the worker. *Practice, 4,* 253–271.

Mullin, V. (2005). Spotlight on consulting issues: Creating psychologically healthier workplaces. *APA Spotlight.* Retrieved from http://www.apa.org/divisions/div13/ Update/2005Fall/2005Fall-Spotlight1.htm

Munson, C. E. (2002). *Handbook of clinical social work supervision.* (3rd ed.). New York: Haworth Press.

National Association of Social Workers. (2008). *Code of ethics of the National Association of Social Workers.* Washington, DC: Author.

National Association of Social Workers. (2001). *NASW Standards for Cultural Competence in Social Work Practice.* Washington, DC: Author.

National Sleep Foundation. (2006). *Sleep–wake cycle: Its physiology and impact on health.* Retrieved from http://www.sleepfoundation.org

Norcross J. C., & Guy, J. D. (2007). *Leaving it at the office: A guide to psychotherapist self-care.* New York: Guilford Press.

Norton, D. (1978). *The dual perspective: inclusion of ethnic minority content in the social work curriculum.* New York: Council of Social Work Education.

O'Brien, A. T., & Haslam, S. A. (2003). *Shaping the future* [Report in response to the issuing of a stress improvement notice from the UK Health and Safety Executive]. Exeter, England: School of Psychology, University of Exeter.

Orem, D. E. (1995). *Nursing concepts of practice* (5th ed.). St Louis: Mosby.

Page, S. (2007). *The difference: How the power of diversity creates better groups, firms, schools, and societies.* Princeton, NJ: Princeton University Press.

Pandy, A., Campbell Quick, J., Rossi, A. M., Nelson, D. L., & Martin, W. (2010). Stress and the workplace: 10 years of science, 1997–2007. In R. Contrada & A. Baum (Eds.), *The handbook of stress science: Biology, psychology, and health* (pp. 137–149). New York: Springer.

Park, C. L. (2010). Making sense of the meaning literature: An integrative review of meaning making and its effects on adjustment to stressful life events. *Psychological Bulletin, 136,* 257–301.

Park, C. L., & Folkman, S. (1997). Meaning in the contest of stress and coping. *Review of General Psychology, 1,* 115–144.

Pearlman, L. A. (1999). Self-care for trauma therapists: Ameliorating vicarious traumatization. In B. H. Stamm (Ed.), *Secondary traumatic stress: Self-care issues for clinicians, researchers, & educators* (pp. 51–64). Lutherville, MD: Sidran Press.

Pearlman, L. A., & Saakvitne, K. W. (1995). Treating therapists with vicarious traumatization and secondary traumatic stress disorders. In C. R. Figley (Ed.), *Compassion fatigue: Coping with secondary traumatic stress disorder in those who treat the traumatized* (pp. 150–177). New York: Brunner-Routledge.

Penny, L. M., & Spector, P. E. (2005). Job stress, incivility, and counterproductive work behavior (CWB): The moderating role of negative affectivity. *Journal of Organizational Behavior, 26*, 777–796.

Peterson, C., & Seligman, M. (1984). Causal explanations as a risk factor for depression: Theory and evidence. *Psychological Review, 91*, 347–374.

Peterson, C., Seligman, M., & Valliant, G. (1988). Pessimistic explanatory style is a risk factor for physical illness: A thirty-five-year longitudinal study. *Journal of Personality and Social Psychology, 55*, 23–27.

Pincus, L. (1997). *An exploratory analysis of the phenomenon of burnout in the school social work profession*. Unpublished doctoral dissertation, New York University, New York.

Prati, G., Pietrantoni, L., & Cicognani, E. (2010). Self-efficacy moderates the relationship between stress appraisal and quality of life among rescue workers. *Anxiety, Stress, & Coping, 23*, 463–470.

Primeau, L. A., & Ferguson, J. M. (1999). Occupational frame of reference. In P. Kramer & J. Hinojosa, *Frames of reference for pediatric occupational therapy* (pp. 469–518). New York: Lippincott, Williams & Wilkins.

Pryce, J. G., Shackelford, K. K., & Pryce, D. H. (2007). *Secondary traumatic stress and the child welfare professional*. Chicago: Lyceum.

Raines, J. C. (1990). Empathy in social work. *Clinical Social Work Journal, 18*, 57–72.

Raver, J. L., & Nishii, L. H. (2010). Once, twice, three times as harmful? Ethnic harassment, gender harassment, and generalized workplace harassment. *Journal of Applied Psychology, 95*, 236–254.

Ray, R., & Schmitt, J. (2007). *No-vacation nation*. [Center for Economic and Policy Research Report]. Retrieved from http://www.cepr.net/index.php/publications/reports/no-vacation-nation/

Ressler, C., & Thompson, J. (2008). *Why work sucks and what you can do about it*. New York: Penguin Group.

Richard, A. A., & Shea, K. (2011). Delineation of self-care and associated concepts. *Journal of Nursing Scholarship, 43*, 255–264.

Robbins, S. (2002). The rush to counsel: Lessons of caution in the aftermath of disaster. *Families in Society, 83*, 113–116.

Rutter, M. (1983). Stress, coping, and development: Some issues and some questions. In N. Garmezy & M. Rutter (Eds.), *Stress, coping, and development in children* (pp. 1–41). New York: McGraw-Hill.

Rycraft, J. (1994). The party isn't over: The agency role in the retention of public child welfare caseworkers. *Social Work, 39*, 75–81.

Saakvitne, K. W., & Pearlman, L. A. (1996). *Transforming the pain: A workbook on vicarious traumatization*. New York: W.W. Norton.

Saakvitne, K. W., Pearlman, L. A., & the Staff of the Traumatic Stress Institute. (1996). *Transforming the pain: A workbook on vicarious traumatization*. New York: W. W. Norton.

Saint-Cyr, Y. (2011). *Federal government launches workplace mental health standards and initiatives.* Retrieved from http://www.slaw.ca/2011/06/23/federal-government-launches-workplace-mental-health-standards-initiative/

Samantrai, K. (1992). Factors in the decision to leave: Retaining social workers with MSWs in public child welfare. *Social Work, 37,* 454–459.

Sapolsky, R. M., (1998). Stress and the maladies of Western life. *Healthline, 17,* 6–7.

Sarker, S., Nicholson, D. B., & Joshi, K. D. (2005). Knowledge transfer in virtual systems development teams: An exploratory study of four key enablers. *IEEE Transactions on Professional Communication, 48,* 201–218.

Schaubroeck, J., & Jones, J. R. (2000). Antecedents of workplace emotional labor dimensions and moderators of their effects on physical symptoms. *Journal of Organizational Behavior, 21,* 163–183.

Schaufeli, W. B., Leiter, M. P., & Maslach, D. (2009). Burnout: 35 years of research and practice. *Career Development Journal, 14,* 204–220.

Schiller, P. L., & Levin, J. S. (1983). Is self-care a social movement? *Social Science & Medicine, 17,* 1342–1352.

Schmitz, J. (2006). *Cultural orientations guide.* (5th ed.). Princeton, NJ: Princeton Training Press.

Schroevers, M. J., & Brandsma, R. (2010). Is learning mindfulness associated with improved affect after mindfulness-based therapy? *British Journal of Psychology, 101,* 95–107.

Schwartz, J. (2004, September 5). Always on the job, employees pay with health. *New York Times* [Online edition]. Retrieved from http://search.proquest.com/docview/432870009?accountid=10346

Seeman, M. (1959). On the meaning of alienation. *American Sociological Review, 24,* 783–791.

Seligman, M.E.P. (2006). *Learned optimism: How to change your mind and your life.* New York: Random House.

Seligman, M.E.P., & Nolen-Hoeksema, S. (1987). Explanatory style and depression. In D. Magnusson & A. Ohman (Eds.), *Psychopathology: An interactional perspective* (pp. 125–139). New York: Academic Press.

Sexton, T. L., & Douglas-Kelley, S. (2010). Finding the common core: Evidence-based practices, clinically relevant evidence, and core mechanisms of change. *Administration and Policy in Mental Health and Mental Health Services Research, 37,* 81–88.

Sholomskas, D. E., Syracuse-Siewert, G., Rounsaville, B. J., Ball, S. A., Nuro, K. F., & Carroll, K. M. (2005). We don't train in vain: A dissemination trial of three strategies of training clinicians in cognitive–behavioral therapy. *Journal of Consulting and Clinical Psychology, 73,* 106–115.

Shulman, L. (2010). *Interactional supervision* (3rd ed.). Washington, DC: NASW Press.

Siegel, R. D. (2010). *The mindfulness solution: Everyday practices for everyday problems.* New York: Guilford Press.

Skovholt, T. M., & Trotter-Mathison, M. (2011). *The resilient practitioner: Burnout prevention and self-care strategies for counselors, therapists, teachers, and mental health professionals* (2nd ed.). New York: Routledge.

Smelser, N. J. (1963). *Theory of collective behavior.* New York: Free Press.

Southern, S. (2007). Countertransference and intersubjectivity: Golden opportunities in clinical supervision. *Sexual Addiction & Compulsivity, 14,* 279–302.

Spreitzer, G., & Porath, C. (2012, January/February). Creating sustainable performance. *Harvard Business Review,* 93–99.

Stahl, B., & Goldstein, E. (2010). *A mindfulness-based stress reduction workbook.* Oakland, CA: New Harbinger Publications.

Stamm, B. H. (2002). *Professional quality of life: Compassion satisfaction and fatigue subscales—III.* Retrieved from http://www.isu.edu/~bhstamm

Takeda, E., Terao, J., Nakaya, Y., Miyamoto, K., Baba, Y., & Chuman, H. (2004). Stress control and human nutrition. *Journal of Investigative Medicine, 51,* 139–145.

Tangri, R. (2003). *Stress costs stress cures: How to recover productivity lost to stress.* Victoria, Canada: Trafford.

Taylor, S. E., Klein, L. C., Lewis, B. P., Gruenwald, T. L., Gurung, R. A. R., & Updegraff, J. A. (2000). Biobehavioral responses to stress in female: Tend-and-befriend, not fight-or-flight. *Psychological Review, 107,* 411–429.

Todd, T. C., & Storm, C. L. (1997). *The complete systemic supervisor: Context, philosophy, and pragmatics.* Boston: Allyn & Bacon.

Trompenaars, F., & Hampden-Turner, C. (1998). *Riding the waves of culture: Understanding diversity in global business* (2nd ed.). New York: McGraw-Hill.

Turner, J. A., Edwards, L. M., Eicken, I. M., Yokoyama, K., Castro, J. R., Tran, A. N., et al. (2005). Intern self-care: An exploratory study into strategy use and effectiveness. *Professional Psychology: Research and Practice, 36,* 674–680.

Van den Broeck, A., Vansteenkiste, M., De Witte, H., & Lens, W. (2008). Explaining the relationship between job characteristics, burnout, and engagement: The role of basic psychological need satisfaction. *Work & Stress, 22,* 277–294.

van der Kolk, B. A., Roth, S., Pelcovitz, D., Sunday, S., & Spinazzola, J. (2005). Disorders of extreme stress: The empirical foundation of a complex adaptation to trauma. *Journal of Traumatic Stress, 18,* 389–399.

van Dernoot Lipsky, L., & Burk, C. (2009). *Trauma stewardship: An everyday guide to caring for self while caring for others.* San Francisco: Berrett-Koehler.

van Heugten, K. (2010). Bullying of social workers: Outcomes of a grounded study into impacts and interventions. *British Journal of Social Work, 40,* 638–655.

Vigoda, E. (2002). Stress-related aftermaths to workplace politics: The relationships among politics, job distress, and aggressive behavior in organizations. *Journal of Organizational Behavior, 23,* 571–591.

Walker, B. (2011). *The anatomy of stretching: Your anatomical guide to flexibility and injury rehabilitation* (2nd ed.). Berkeley, CA: North Atlantic Books.

Walsh, R. (2011). Lifestyle and mental health. *American Psychologist, 66,* 579–592.

Watzlawick, P, Weakland, J., & Fitsch R. (1974). *Change: Principles of problem formation and problem resolution.* New York: W. W. Norton.

Weinbach. R. W. (2008). *The social worker as manager: A practical guide to success.* Boston: Pearson Education.

Welbourne, J. L., Eggerth, D., Hartley, T. A., Andrew, M. E., & Sanchez, F. (2007). Coping strategies in the workplace: Relationships with attributional style and job satisfaction. *Journal of Vocational Behavior, 70,* 312–325.

Whitaker, T. (2008). *Who wants to be a social worker? Career influences and timing.* [NASW Membership Workforce Study]. Washington, DC: National Association of Social Workers.

White, M. L., Peters, R., & Schim, S. (2011). Spirituality and self-care. *Nursing Science Quarterly, 24,* 48–56.

Williams, I. D., Richardson, T. A., Moore, D. D., Eubanks Gamble, L., & Keeling, M. L. (2010). Perspectives on self-care. *Journal of Creativity in Mental Health, 5,* 320–338.

Wilson, J. P., Lindy, J. D., & Raphael, B. (1994). Empathic strain and therapist defense: Type I and II CTSs. In J. P. Wilson & J. D. Lindy (Eds.), *Countertransference in the treatment of PTSD* (pp. 31–61). New York: Guilford Press.

Yassen, J. (1995). Preventing secondary traumatic stress disorder. In C. R. Figley (Ed.), *Compassion fatigue: Coping with secondary traumatic stress disorder in those who treat the traumatized* (pp. 178–208). New York: Brunner-Routledge.

Yollin, P. (2011, June 5). Pain doctor identifies with suffering patients. *San Francisco Chronicle,* A1, A14.

Index

In this index, *f* denotes figure.